13 CRUCIAL
QUESTIONS
JESUS
WANTS
TO ASK YOU

Also by Tom Carter

Spurgeon's Commentary on Great Chapters of the Bible

13 CRUCIAL QUESTIONS JESUS WANTS TO ASK YOU

TOM CARTER

kregel
PUBLICATIONS

Grand Rapids, MI 49501

13 Crucial Questions Jesus Wants to Ask You

Published by Kregel Publications, a division of Kregel, Inc., P.O. Box 2607, Grand Rapids, MI 49501. Kregel Publications provides trusted, biblical publications for Christian growth and service. Your comments and suggestions are valued.

Cover and book design: Nicholas G. Richardson

Library of Congress Cataloging-in-Publication Data
Carter, Tom.
    13 crucial questions Jesus wants to ask you / by Tom Carter.
       p.   cm.
    1. Jesus Christ—Miscellanea. 2. Jesus Christ—Words.
I. Title.
BT306.C365   1999   232—dc21   98-53734
                                                          CIP
ISBN 0-8254-2359-7

Printed in the United States

2 3 / 04 03 02 01 00

Contents

5

Introduction

ALMOST EVERYONE HAS A question they'd like to ask Jesus.

"Why did You let my baby die?"
"Where were You when I was being sexually abused all those years?"
"How can You love a sinner like me?"
"Can my wife in heaven see me now?"
"How could You have no beginning?"
"If You know all my needs, what's the point of my telling them to You in prayer?"

Did you ever stop to think that Jesus has some questions for you? In the pages ahead we will wrestle with thirteen of them. Our Lord originally asked these questions during His ministry on earth, and they are recorded in the New Testament. But because Scripture is the living Word of God, we can put ourselves in the sandals of the original people who were cornered by these questions. Some were posed to individuals, others to the disciples, and still others to those who conspired against Jesus. The question in chapter 2 was submitted to the heavenly Father. Though it was not strictly asked of any human being, Jesus surely wants us to grapple with it. In each case, therefore, we can assume that these are questions Jesus wants to ask us.

Fasten your seat belt, because these are not soft questions. Some are confrontational, others challenging, and still others are humbling, personal, and breathtaking. All of them are crucial to a Christian's spiritual growth. So let's get ready to listen, learn, and respond.

1

A FUNDAMENTAL QUESTION:

"Who do you say that I am?"
(Matt. 16:15)

VINCE LOMBARDI, THE FAMOUS head coach of the Green Bay Packers, once watched his team suffer a humiliating defeat to an underdog opponent. The next day before practice, he picked up a football, held it up to his players, including some pro-bowl veterans, and said, "Gentlemen, this is a football." Coach Lombardi figured it was time to call his team back to the fundamentals.

After teaching His disciples for nearly three years, Jesus paused to ask them this fundamental question: "Who do you say that I am?" (Matt. 16:15). Today we must still begin right there. Before we can think properly about anything else in Scripture—including salvation—we must know the person of Christ.

Pollster George Gallup once asked a random sample of Americans, "Who do you say that Jesus is?" Most everyone described Him in positive terms, using such words as "loving," "forgiving," "kind," and "compassionate." Forty-two percent said that Christ was "God among people." That is the biblical view, and I'm surprised that so many people espoused it. The others in the survey looked upon Jesus as a great leader, a teacher of morals, or a prophet. The common denominator in those statements is that Jesus was only a man.

If someone else went around and asked people, "Who do you say that I am?" we'd think that he or she was insecure. But Jesus asked this question for the sake of our eternal security. In John 8:24 He told the Jews, "Unless you believe that I am He [the divine Lord], you will die in your sins." John 17:3 teaches that knowing the Son is the essence of eternal life. And Romans 10:9 says, "If you confess with your mouth Jesus as

Lord, and believe in your heart that God raised Him from the dead, you will be saved." Therefore, nothing less than our salvation hinges on our answer to the fundamental question of Christ's identity.

WHO'S WHO AMONG THE JEWS

Before asking His disciples who they thought He was, our Lord asked, "Who do people say that the Son of Man is?" (Matt. 16:13). I think Jesus was warning His disciples against the misleading notions that people had about Him. After all, when you're on the lookout for land mines, you're less likely to step on one.

The disciples responded: "Some say John the Baptist; and others, Elijah; but still others, Jeremiah, or one of the prophets" (v. 14). This answer reflected the common notion that Jesus was one of the great prophets who had come back to life. Perhaps this mistaken idea was based on Deuteronomy 18:18, which said that God would one day raise up a prophet like Moses among the people.

When Herod first heard about Jesus, the tetrarch "said to his servants, 'This is John the Baptist; he has risen from the dead'" (Matt. 14:2). Like John the Baptist, Jesus preached the kingdom of God and boldly challenged people to repent of their sins. But John was merely a voice calling people to prepare themselves spiritually for the advent of Christ, whereas Jesus was the Lord Himself (see Isa. 40:3; John 1:23). R. V. G. Tasker wrote, "John could prepare men to receive the reign of God in their hearts, but he [Jesus] could enable them to receive it. He [John] stood on the threshold of the kingdom of God, but Jesus was the door through whom men alone could enter it."[1]

Others looked upon Jesus as Elijah who had returned from heaven. Malachi 4:5 had said that Elijah would be sent by God "before the coming of the great and terrible day of the LORD." Jews today traditionally set an empty chair and place setting for Elijah at the seder (Passover) meal. Elijah's distinguishing trait was his ability to perform miracles. For example, he multiplied the last bit of flour and oil of a widow and her son so that they could eat for many days (1 Kings 17:12–15). That reminds us of Jesus' feeding five thousand men (not counting the women and children; Matt. 14:21) from five barley loaves and two fish (John 6:5–13).

Both Elijah and Jesus restored a dead boy to life (1 Kings 17:17–24; Luke 7:11–15). Elijah called down fire from heaven to consume a burnt offering (1 Kings 18:30–39), and in a similar manner Jesus' words set listeners' hearts ablaze (Luke 24:32). Elijah divided the waters of the Jordan so that he and Elisha could cross over on dry ground (2 Kings 2:8), and Jesus walked on water (Matt. 14:25).

From what has been said about Elijah, we can understand how the crowds could have been confused about Jesus' identity. But though there were similarities between the two men, Jesus was not Elijah. The latter was only a spokesperson for God, whereas Jesus was God incarnate and the Messiah of the world (John 1:1–18; 20:31).

Others in Jesus' day viewed Him as Jeremiah. Again, we can see some resemblance between the ministries of Jeremiah and of Jesus. For example, Jeremiah was known as the weeping prophet. In fact, his book of "Lamentations" expressed his intense sorrow over the Babylonians' destruction of Jerusalem. This was due to the Israelites' violation of the Mosaic covenant. Likewise, Jesus was filled with anguish over the calamity that awaited Jerusalem at the hands of the Romans (Luke 19:41). Christ was also grieved over the people's rejection of Him as the Messiah.

Both Jeremiah and Jesus were misunderstood and persecuted by the people of their day. Jeremiah wrote about the new covenant, in which God would spiritually write His law on the hearts of His people and forgive their sins (Jer. 31:33–34). But Jesus fulfilled the new covenant by dying on the cross, where He endured God's wrath and offered Himself as the atoning sacrifice for our sins (Mark 15:34; 1 John 2:2).

The common thread running through John the Baptist, Elijah, and Jeremiah was their prophetic voice. They were spokespersons for God. But Christ was the God about whom they spoke. The prophets were messengers, but Jesus was the message.

The survey of opinions about Jesus read like an ancient *Who's Who*. Yet the popular notions still fell short, for they included no mention of Jesus as the Messiah. The various views recorded in Matthew 16:14 tell us something about the people who held them, but nothing about the true identity of Christ. This verse reveals that the people of Jesus' day had absolutely no clue that He was the Savior of the world (1 John 4:14).

COUNTERFEIT CHRISTS

Still today, public opinion about Jesus is untrustworthy. Rumors, surveys, or polls will always carry with them subtle deceptions. It will never do to take a vote on who Jesus is. It may look as if society holds high opinions about Christ, but all those views, if they aren't the right one, not only miss the mark but insult our Lord. Tragically, countless people form in their minds a picture of Christ based on what others have said about Him rather than on what Scripture has testified about Him. Don't let that happen to you. Don't base your ideas about Jesus on anything less than the inspired Word of God.

Over the centuries the counterfeit understandings of Jesus have fallen into three categories. One is the idea that He was God who only looked like man. Cerinthus, a contemporary of the apostle John, was the leader of a cult that fell into this error. They called themselves "docetists" from a Greek word meaning "to seem." They believed Jesus *seemed* human but wasn't. Thus, they denied the incarnation of Christ. John warned against docetism when he wrote in 1 John 4:2–3, "Every spirit that confesses that Jesus Christ has come in the flesh is from God; and every spirit that does not confess Jesus is not from God; and this is the spirit of the antichrist."

Today some well-meaning people make a similar mistake when they campaign for the deity of Christ at the expense of His humanity. They wince at the mention of Jesus being tempted, exhausted, hungry, thirsty, and in pain. To be sure, we must defend the doctrine of Christ's deity against those who would deny it. But to scrimp on His humanity is to be guilty of heresy.

A second misconception about Jesus is that, though He holds a special position next to God, He is still only a created being. In the fourth century A.D., Arius taught that only the heavenly Father is eternal. Jesus supposedly was His first and greatest creation, who in turn created the universe. In A.D. 325, the Nicene Council condemned Arianism, but for another 250 years the Arians continued to plague the church with this blasphemy, and the idea still infects several theologies. Such cults as the Mormons and the Jehovah's Witnesses believe that Christ is secondary to God as a created being.

The third pitfall that has tripped many an unwary seeker of truth is the teaching that Jesus was nothing more than a man. The first-century Jewish leaders believed this so firmly that they crucified Christ for claiming to be God (see Mark 14:61–64; John 10:33). In 1906 the eminent German medical missionary and theologian Albert Schweitzer wrote a book entitled *The Quest for the Historical Jesus*.[2] Schweitzer argued that Jesus was deceived about Himself. Schweitzer also claimed that people were mistaken who believed that Christ was divine. In 1952, Schweitzer was awarded the Nobel Peace Prize, but he serves as a reminder to us of the fallibility of our most respected and honored religious leaders.

These three commonly held erroneous views about Christ reveal the inadequacy of public opinion. Humanity's best thinking will always fall short of giving Christ the glory He deserves. The only trustworthy testimony is that of the Bible. When you stake your life on it, you won't go wrong about Jesus.

PETER'S CONCLUSION

After hearing what the crowds thought about Him, Jesus asked His disciples, "But who do you say that I am?" (Matt. 16:15). I heard about a young seminary graduate who was being tested by his ordination council. They fired all kinds of theological questions at him. They asked him what he believed concerning the inspiration and authority of Scripture, the person of Christ, the Holy Spirit, the nature of the church, and a host of other theological issues. After each question, he replied, "Dr. Strong says. . . ." He was quoting Augustus Strong, who wrote a classic text on systematic theology.[3]

The council was pleased with all his answers and voted to grant him ordination. After the meeting, the chairman complimented the pastor-to-be: "Your beliefs are as straight as an arrow, as solid as they come!"

The young man replied, "I don't believe any of those things. I was only quoting Dr. Strong, because I knew that's what you wanted to hear." To say the least, the ordination council was heartsick to hear that admission.

Jesus likewise has no desire to hear us talk about what our parents, our pastors, or our churches believe. He wants us to believe the truth of God's Word that He is "the Christ, the Son of God" (John 20:31).

In Matthew 16:15, the Greek pronoun rendered "you" is in an emphatic position. The verse literally reads, "But you, whom do you say Me to be?" Jesus was implying, "Are you willing to stand alone in your estimation of Me? Do you dare take the risk of breaking away from public opinion and hold a contrary personal conviction about Me?"

Peter Marshall, the late chaplain to the United States Senate, once prayed these words on behalf of the nation's leaders: "Give us clear vision, O God, that we may know where to stand and what to stand for, because unless we stand for something, we shall fall for anything." Marshall understood the indispensability of personal convictions.

A conviction is a belief that people can't help sharing. As I get acquainted with people—often those who have visited my church—I ask them, "What does Jesus mean to you?" or "Where do you stand with Christ?" Every now and then an embarrassed look comes over the other person's face, and he or she replies, "That's a personal matter between God and me. I'd rather not talk about it."

Our relationship with Christ should be personal. But it must also be something we are willing—even eager—to share. Jesus asked His disciples to respond openly to the question, "Who do you say that I am?" Elsewhere Scripture commands us, "Always be prepared to give an answer to everyone who asks you to give the reason for the hope that you have" (1 Peter 3:15 NIV).

Evidently all twelve disciples answered Jesus' question in Matthew 16:13 (see v. 14). But when He asked, "Who do you say that I am?" only Peter had the courage to say, "You are the Christ, the Son of the living God" (v. 16).

According to John 1:41, the word *Christ* means "Messiah." The Messiah is the key figure in Old Testament prophecy. As early as Genesis 3:15, God had promised to send a Deliverer who would crush Satan's head. Isaiah pictured Him as our Substitute, who would carry the weight of the world's sins (Isa. 53:6). Daniel counted the years before the Messiah's coming (Dan. 9:24–26), and Micah foretold the Messiah's place of birth (Mic. 5:2). Thus Peter, by calling Jesus "the Christ" (Matt. 16:16), was in effect saying, "You are the One for whom Israel has waited for centuries, and the One about whom the prophets spoke. You are the hope of all the world!"

Peter declared Jesus to be Messiah and "the Son of the living God." Today Christians are spiritual children of the living God only by adoption. Romans 8:15 makes this clear: "You have received a spirit of adoption as sons." Jesus is the "Son of God" (John 20:31) in His natural and intimate relationship with the Father (see Mark 5:7; Luke 1:35). The title indicates that Christ is not only to be identified with the Father but also is fully and absolutely equal with Him (see John 5:18; 10:30, 36). Hence, Peter's words in Matthew 16:16 place Jesus in a class by Himself. The disciples' statement implies that no person—not even a prophet—is worthy to be compared with Him.

Napoleon is reported to have said: "All the heroes of antiquity were men, and I am a man. But no one is like Jesus Christ. He is more than a man."

Jesus Is Lord in Sin City

Matthew 16:13 informs us that Jesus asked His probing question while in "the district of Caesarea Philippi." The inhabitants of the city were notorious for their worship of the fertility god of the Canaanites, Baal, and the Roman god of fertility, Pan. Herod later built a temple in Caesarea Philippi for the worship of Caesar. In the midst of all this idolatry, Jesus asked His disciples, "Who do you say that I am?" (v. 15). And Peter replied, "The Christ, the Son of the living God" (v. 16).

Rather than Caesarea Philippi, Jesus today might take us to a place such as Las Vegas, which epitomizes worldliness and idolizes the love for money. Perhaps while leading us down the main boulevards of the city, with their glittering casinos all around, Jesus would ask us, "Who do you say that I am?" Then He would wait for us to reply, "You are the light of the world!"

Or maybe Jesus would take us to a Superbowl football game, with its overdone razzle-dazzle displays that encourage us to worship sports. I can imagine Jesus guiding us to the best seat in the stadium, in the midst of tens of thousands of delirious fans and hundreds of millions more around the world watching the game on television. He would wait until the game's final moments, when one team, perhaps behind by five points, launches a desperation pass sixty yards from the goal line. The receiver makes a diving catch in the end zone to win the game. The fans spring to their feet and let out a roar that can be heard miles away. Jesus at that second would turn to us to ask, "Who do you say that I am?" He would expect us to reply, "My only object of worship!"

I thoroughly enjoy the entire football season. I remember reading to our children from a Bible storybook. The story was about idols, and I asked our kids, "What is an idol?" Our seven-year-old answered, "A statue." Then my wife asked, "What are some idols that people love more than Jesus today?" Our little girl gave me a side glance and answered, "Football."

My first reaction was to reply at once, "No, no—I don't worship football!" But I resisted the urge, calmed down, and said, "You've got a point there. If I'm not careful, watching football games can become more important than Jesus."

Consider one more example of worldly idolatry—Hollywood's Academy Awards. Adoring fans glue themselves to their television sets while screen idols, decked out in outrageous apparel, promenade from limousines into the auditorium. During the evening, one movie star after another make speeches that reflect undivided devotion to the motion picture industry. The Oscars seem to be the most prestigious and coveted awards the world has to offer. I can imagine Jesus waiting behind stage to meet the winners of the Oscars for best actor and best actress. But He is not waiting to congratulate them. Instead, as they walk offstage with thunderous applause still ringing in their ears and their faces flushed with a once-in-a-lifetime emotion, Jesus asks them, "Who do you say that I am?" And He expects them to answer, "My Lord and my God!"

It was in a first-century setting where pagan temples and idols abounded that Jesus asked His disciples, "Who do you say that I am?" And Peter declared, "Thou art the Christ, the Son of the living God." What a victory, Peter! This was your greatest moment!

Action Steps

During my teenage years, I was among a group of Christians enjoying a campfire on the beach in Santa Cruz, California. As we sat there after a day of swimming in the ocean, our leader retold the story of Jesus asking His disciples, "Who do you say that I am?" The leader then invited us to answer that question. One by one voices replied, "Lord Jesus, You're my Savior . . . the Love of my life . . . my friend . . . my Lord . . . my God . . . my Everything . . . the One who pleads for me at the heavenly Father's right hand . . . my King . . . my Redeemer . . . the Rock on which I stand. . . ." I'll never forget that inspirational evening!

Now it's your turn to answer Jesus' question. If from your heart you can reply, "Jesus, You are my Lord, my God, and my all," then you know what life and eternity are all about.

But this question should do more than just bring you to Christ. Let it compel you to brings others to the Savior. Do you teach a Bible study? Do you witness to others? Are you active in church life? Great! But what is your purpose in doing these things? Is it just to instill truth in others? Don't forget that Jesus said, "I am . . . the truth" (John 14:6). The first goal of our Christian service is not to impart knowledge, to enlighten inquiring minds, or to train people to live in a way that pleases God. Rather, it is to bring spiritually lost people into a personal relationship with the living Christ. If you already know Him as Savior and Lord, your aim should be to exalt Him so that your love for Christ glows to a red-hot brilliance. As John Wesley once said, "Get on fire for God, and people will come to watch you burn."

Is Jesus worth all that time and effort? Does He deserve your unlimited service, your uncompromising testimony, your unrivaled love, and your unconditional worship? That depends on your answer to this question: Who do you say Jesus is?

Study Guide

1. Why is it essential that everyone understand who Jesus is?

2. Isaiah 9:6 provides at least four answers to the question, "Who is Jesus Christ?" Find His titles in this verse and describe in your own words what they mean.

3. In each of the verses below, who did Jesus' enemies say He was?

   • Matthew 27:37

   • Mark 1:24

   • Mark 5:7

4. In the following verses what did Jesus claim about Himself?

   • John 10:30

   • John 10:36

   • John 13:13

5. What practical lessons do you learn from Jesus' "I am" statements in the following verses?

   • John 6:35

   • John 8:12

   • John 8:58

   • John 10:9

   • John 10:11

   • John 11:25

   • John 14:6

   • John 15:1

6. Who did the following people say Jesus was?

   • John the Baptist—John 1:29

   • Nathanael—John 1:49

   • Martha—John 11:27

- Thomas—John 20:28

- John—John 20:31

7. For centuries people have debated whether Jesus is God. How does each verse below affirm the deity of Christ?

   - Matthew 1:23

   - John 10:30

   - John 14:9

   - Acts 20:28

   - Romans 9:5

   - Colossians 2:9

   - Titus 2:13

   - Hebrews 1:3

   - Hebrews 1:8

   - Hebrews 13:8

   - 2 Peter 1:1

8. If someone asked you, "Who is Jesus Christ?" what would be your answer?

A PROFOUND QUESTION:

"My God, My God, why hast Thou forsaken Me?" (Matt. 27:46)

ON JANUARY 15, 1991, the following letter appeared in the syndicated newspaper column "Dear Abby":

Dear Abby,

I am troubled with something a reader wrote: "What right do we mortals have to demand an explanation from God?" Abby, that writer has never known the gut-wrenching pain of losing a child.

In 1988, my beautiful 22-year-old daughter was killed by a drunken driver. At first, I screamed, "He not only killed her, he killed me too—only I can't die!"

I then got on my knees and begged God: "You can do anything. You can perform miracles. You can bring my daughter back to life. Please, God, let me trade places with her—please let me lie in that coffin, and let her out to live her life. She has never been married or experienced the miracle of being a mother. I am old. I have lived. I've had my chance at life, but she hasn't. Please, please, let me trade places with her. . . . She didn't deserve to die!"

As you can see, Abby, I'm still here—and not because I want to be, either. Mostly because I didn't have the guts to pull the trigger or take the pills to get me out of the terrible pain and loss I live with every minute of my life.

God didn't see fit to bargain with me. . . . The drunk who killed my precious daughter (and me, too) spent less than six months behind bars. Today, he walks in the sun while my little girl is in a dark grave—with no sun. And though I also walk in the sun, my heart and soul are in that dark grave with her.

God didn't answer my prayers, and I resent being told that I have no right to question God. If there is a God, and if I ever get to meet Him face to face, you can bet your life I will have plenty of whys for Him to answer. . . . I am mad that I am having to live in a world where she no longer lives, and I want to know why. Why shouldn't I have the right to ask God?

Signed, a bereaved mother.

Admit it. You also have wanted to ask God similar questions, though perhaps not as strongly as that grieving mother. It may have been when your fiancé(e) broke the marriage engagement, or your spouse divorced you, or your daughter was raped, or cancer threatened your life, or thieves broke into your house and stole a precious possession.

At the age of seventeen I was diagnosed with diabetes. My physician explained, "Your pancreas is no longer working, but you cannot live without the insulin it produces. So you must inject yourself with insulin twice a day for the rest of your life. You will need to test your body's sugar level before each meal and at bedtime. It is crucial that you eat properly and never miss a meal or an injection."

I did some research on my own and learned that, even while maintaining tight control of my disease, I was a higher-than-average risk for blindness, heart disease, and strokes later in life. I couldn't help asking God why.

At first I felt guilty about doing that. But now I'm convinced there is no sin involved in this question—as long as it represents the honest pursuit of faith, rather than bitterness. While suspended on Calvary's cross, Jesus Himself asked God why, and in high decibels. He "cried out with a loud voice, . . . 'My God, My God, why hast Thou forsaken Me?'" (Matt. 27:46).

Surely no sentence ever fell from human lips that contains more anguish in it than this one. All of Jesus' other recorded questions were designed to teach His disciples, arouse the interest of the crowds, or confront His enemies. But our Lord raised this profound question for His own sake. It teaches us five powerful lessons:

JESUS TOOK THE PUNISHMENT FOR OUR SINS

Second Corinthians 5:21 states that God made Jesus "who knew no sin to be sin on our behalf, that we might become the righteousness of God in Him." Here is one simple reason the Father forsook His Son on the cross. Jesus, though absolutely holy, shouldered the consequences of sin and the righteous wrath of God deserved by sinners. Isaiah 53:6 says, "The LORD has caused the iniquity of us all to fall on Him."

Some Bible scholars claim that Jesus only felt forsaken, that in fact the heavenly Father was right by Christ's side all along. For example, T. R. Glover remarked, "I have sometimes thought there never was an utterance that reveals more amazingly the distance between feeling and fact."[1] But because this view makes our Lord guilty of speaking an untruth about the Father, it must be rejected.

David observed in Psalm 37:25, "I have not seen the righteous forsaken." Yet Jesus—the supremely righteous One—was forsaken by God so that we might never be forsaken. While Stephen, the first recorded Christian martyr, was being stoned, he saw heaven open up and the Lord Jesus ready to welcome him home (Acts 7:55–56). Yet while Jesus was dying, heaven was locked shut against Him. God utterly abandoned His Son to the mockery, suffering, shame, and horror of the cross.

After Jesus was tempted by Satan, angels ministered to Him (Matt. 4:11). And while Jesus agonized in Gethsemane over His upcoming death, an angel was sent to strengthen Him (Luke 22:43). But apparently there were no angels by Jesus' side when He hung on the cross. Even the Holy Spirit had been withdrawn. Talk about leaving someone in the lurch! God left Jesus to drink to the dregs His eternal wrath.

Galatians 3:13 calls what Jesus experienced a curse: "Christ redeemed us from the curse of the Law, having become a curse for us—for it is written, 'Cursed is everyone who hangs on a tree.'" We deserved to bear the eternal punishment for violating the law of God, but Jesus did so for us. Because Christ, as our sinless Substitute, allowed Himself to be deserted by the Father, we can claim by faith the promise of Hebrews 13:5: "I will never desert you, nor will I ever forsake you."

Felipe Garza was a normal fifteen-year-old boy from Patterson, California. For example, he did chores on his father's farm after school. There was nothing noteworthy about his simple life, that is, until he literally gave his heart to his girlfriend, who was in need of a transplant. In January of 1994, Felipe told his mother he was going to die and that he wanted his girlfriend, Donna Ashlock, to receive his heart. Three weeks later a blood vessel unexpectedly burst in Felipe's brain, killing him instantly. Donna received his heart—and a new lease on life. She later said, "I will never forget Felipe. I will always love him for this."

Less than three years later, Donna also died. Her boyfriend Felipe had given her temporary life. But when Jesus took our place on Calvary's cross, He made eternal life possible for us! Because He was forsaken by God for a time, we can enjoy an eternity in heaven with the Lord. Because Jesus endured God's wrath, we can be pardoned. Because Jesus paid the price for our sin, we can be freed from its bondage in our thoughts, words, and actions.

SIN SEPARATES US FROM GOD

Jesus' profound question in Matthew 27:46 also stamps this truth on our hearts with indelible ink—sin separates people from God. Isaiah 59:2 couldn't be more plain if it were printed on a billboard: "Your iniquities have made a separation between you and your God." Romans 6:23 makes a similar point: "The wages of sin is death." In this verse, *death* means a separation from God, an end to every purpose for which God created us. It is not only the termination of physical life but also eternal separation from God.

Why do non-Christians reject the claims of Christ? Because they are far from God. Why do they say, "I can't see Jesus at work in my life"? Because they are distant from Him. How is it that we believers can lose our joy, cease praying, and neglect our Bibles? Because we have entertained sin in our hearts, and sin will always separate us from God. Why do we grow indifferent toward the plight of the spiritually lost? Because sin has driven us from the heart of a caring heavenly Father. Sin works to accomplish its deadly goal subtly, quietly, and unnoticeably.

Why do some Christians drop out of the church? I have heard many excuses: "The church is filled with hypocrites." "I am not spiritually fed there." "No one cares about me there." "The church is out of touch."

Sometimes these criticisms are valid. But I always come back to the truth of Hebrews 10:25: "Let us not neglect our church meetings, as some people do" (LB). During the years of Jesus' earthly ministry, the synagogue was jam-packed with self-righteous scribes and Pharisees. Nevertheless, it was our Lord's habit to worship in the synagogue on the Sabbath (see Luke 4:16).

The real reason Christians separate themselves from the church is that sin has separated them from the Lord. What is the church but the body of Christ? Lack of fellowship with the body of believers is a symptom of loss of fellowship with its head—Jesus Christ (Eph. 1:22–23). If the Father abandoned His holy Son when He bore our sins on the cross, the Father will certainly withdraw from fellowship with us when we sin against Him.

GOD IS HOLY

Why did the Father have to forsake His Son? It is because God's "eyes are too pure to look on evil," and He "cannot tolerate wrong" (Hab. 1:13 NIV). Donald Grey Barnhouse once wrote, "The people who teach that God is love without teaching that God is also hate of sin, have, in reality, another god who is Satan with a mask on."[2]

Imagine an orchestra playing before a concert audience with one instrument out of tune. The conductor has no choice but to ask that one musician to leave. Likewise, when the crucified Christ bore our sins, He became "out of tune" with the Father, so God had to forsake Him.

The disciples deserted Jesus because of fear. The demons turned against Him out of hatred. Jealousy drove the religious leaders to plot against Him. But the Father forsook the Son because of holiness. Once Jesus bore our sins on the cross, our holy God had to abandon Him completely.

Here is a wonderful lesson for us. To grow in holiness, we must also forsake anything that will lead us into sin. The Bible warns us that those who are not holy will not see the Lord (Heb. 12:14). If the Father, due to His holiness, had to abandon His Son when He bore our sins on the cross, we can't turn our hearts toward worldly pursuits without the stench of sin rubbing off on us. Sin immediately drives us from fellowship with our holy God.

Some time ago a young Christian man confessed to me that he had committed a colossal mistake by marrying the wrong woman. He was anxious to correct his error by divorcing his new wife, whom he had not really known very long, and marrying his longtime girlfriend. He asked me, "How will Christians feel about me if I do this?" I told him that he should be more concerned with how God would feel about it. In frustration he replied, "But I can't be happy as long as I'm married to the wrong woman."

"God can make the wrong wife the right one," I said to encourage him. "Instead of taking *you* out of the problem, your Lord wants to take *the problem* out of you. Trust Him to change your heart and give you love for your wife." But I had to add, "Even if you can't be happy with your wife, the Christian's true goal in life is not happiness but holiness. Marriage is a sacred union, and God expects you to honor it."

The young man agreed to practice obedience. He eventually began to find joy in his wife. God was rewarding his pursuit of holiness!

A holy God had no other choice but to forsake Jesus when He became our sinless Substitute. Christ's sacrifice made it possible for us to fellowship with our holy God (1 John 1:3). And "like the Holy One who called you, be holy yourselves also in all your behavior" (1 Peter 1:15). You can do that by forsaking anything that carries the scent of sin.

JESUS PROVED HIS LOVE FOR US

"Greater love has no one than this, that one lay down his life for his friends" (John 15:13). On the cross Jesus laid down not only His life, but also His soul. From all eternity His fellowship with the Father had been unbroken. As the opening of John's gospel states, "He was in the beginning with God" (1:2). During Jesus' earthly ministry, He was able to say that the Father "has not left Me alone" (John 8:29), and that "the Father is with Me" (John 16:32). But at Calvary, the eternal fellowship between the Father and the Son came to an abrupt halt. The wedge of our sin drove an impassable barrier between the Messiah and His heavenly Father.

My favorite time of day is the moment I arrive home in the evening to my wife and three children. I love to hear the kids shout, "Daddy's home!"—especially when they say it with joy rather than dread—which is most of the time! Sometimes they are playing in the front yard, and when I pull into the driveway, they surround my car with smiles, love, and exciting reports of their adventures that day.

The thought of being separated from my family causes me to shudder. I remained single until age thirty-two, and I would never want to return to that. I have lost time to make up! Being away from my wife and children for a week while on a ministry assignment is bad enough. But for eternity? Forget it! I wouldn't give up the closeness we share for anything. Jesus, however, surrendered His intimacy with God. Love for us compelled Jesus to endure the darkness, the pain, the loneliness, and the sorrow of being forsaken by His Father.

You may ask, "How bad could Christ's separation from God be when it lasted only a short while?" It's much worse than any of us could ever imagine. Granted, Jesus was eventually reunited in fellowship with His heavenly Father. We can infer this from such passages as Luke 23:43. But though God abandoned our Lord for only a relatively brief period of time, the eternal punishment meant for all humankind was unleashed on Christ. Somehow during Jesus' crucifixion, He suffered our eternal punishment. Those who die in a state of unbelief will be punished for their own sins, but Jesus paid the price for the sins of the human race. And love drove Him to make that sacrifice.

UNBELIEVERS WILL BE ETERNALLY SEPARATED FROM GOD

What is hell? Jesus called it the place of "outer darkness" (Matt. 8:12) and an "eternal fire" (18:8). It is the place where "there shall be weeping and gnashing of teeth" (13:42), and "where their worm does not die" (Mark 9:48a). Revelation portrays hell as a place where Satan and his demonic cohorts "will be tormented day and night forever and ever" (20:10). These are appalling descriptions indeed. But if we had to melt them all down to one, we could say that hell is the place of eternal separation from God.

Jesus warned that at the final judgment He will say to some, "Depart from Me, you who practice lawlessness" (Matt. 7:23). On another occasion He made a similar pronouncement: "Depart from Me, accursed ones" (25:41). Paul testified that "the penalty of eternal destruction" is to be "away from the presence of the Lord" (2 Thess. 1:9). That banishment from the Lord's presence will be indescribable and irrecoverable.

In this life no one is completely God-forsaken. Even such monsters as Adolf Hitler or Saddam Hussein have received the Lord's daily gifts of health and life. You may feel as though God has left you in the lurch. But if for one moment you could see eternal judgment in its true light, you would realize that the Father is now closer to you than your own breath.

We cherish notions of independence. In our human nature we want God off our back. But if we could fathom the depth of Jesus' one unanswered question recorded in Matthew 27:46, the hair on the back of the neck of even the most hardened unbeliever would stand on end at the mention of the word "condemnation." Surely the Spirit wants the appalling thought of unbelievers standing on the verge of eternal separation from Christ to kindle in us a zeal to share the gospel with them.

Some people you know couldn't care less if they are forsaken by God. That's why they need you to care for them. More than that, they need you to pray for them and share Christ with them.

Action Steps

When God the Father abandoned His Son on the cross, Jesus experienced the summit of suffering and the apex of anguish. Matthew 27:45 tells us that from noon until 3 P.M. "darkness fell upon all the land." During that foreboding time, our Lord cried, "My God, My God, why hast Thou forsaken Me?" By asking this question, Jesus was turning *to* the Father, not *away* from Him, for Christ believed that even in the darkness of His anguish He could seek God and find Him again!

Remember that truth in your hour of darkness. Even then call out in prayer to the Lord, for He cares for you and is yours. He will answer you because He forsook your sinless Substitute—Jesus Christ—on the cross. When you feel abandoned by God, don't scoff at Scripture and pass over prayer. Instead, remind yourself of this invitation: "Let us therefore draw near with confidence to the throne of grace, that we may receive mercy and may find grace to help in time of need" (Heb. 4:16). We can do that, because we have a great high priest who can sympathize with our weakness (vv. 14–15).

Jesus' cry of anguish in Matthew 27:46 was not His final statement from the cross. Just before He gave up His life, He prayed, "Father, into Thy hands I commit My spirit" (Luke 23:46; see John 19:30). Our Lord reached a point when He stopped asking God why and simply trusted Him for the unexplained. As 1 Peter 2:23 explains, "And while being reviled, He did not revile in return; while suffering, He uttered no threats, but kept entrusting Himself to Him who judges righteously."

Dare to trust God that much. Earlier I said there is no sin involved in asking God why, as long as the question is the inquiry of faith. But even then, there comes a time when you must put aside your curiosity and rest in the wisdom of your heavenly Father. In heaven all your questions will be answered. So stop punishing yourself with nagging doubts about why a drunk driver killed your child, why cancer took the life of your spouse, or why you had to suffer through an unwanted divorce.

If you claim to trust God for your soul, prove it by trusting Him for your unanswered questions. Say, "Father, into Your hands I commit my broken heart." Then, as He did with Jesus, the heavenly Father will reach out to you, wrap you in His arms, and gather you to Himself.

Study Guide

1. Jesus' words in Matthew 27:46 were uttered previously by David in Psalm 22:1. David also felt forsaken by God. Describe a time when you felt that God had deserted you. What was the outcome?

2. Share an experience when you yearned to ask God why He had allowed something disappointing or tragic to happen to you or to someone you loved.

3. Our holy God forsook Jesus on the cross because He became our sinless Substitute (2 Cor. 5:21; see Hab. 1:13). From this we see that God cannot tolerate sin. In each of the following verses, look for the word "sin," and then write down the warning given about it.

• Numbers 32:23

• Isaiah 59:2

• Romans 6:23

• Romans 14:23

• Hebrews 3:13

• Hebrews 11:25

• Hebrews 12:1

• James 4:17

4. Hebrews 12:2 says that Jesus, "for the joy set before Him endured the cross." Because of the joy of accomplishing the Father's will and being exalted to the Father's right hand, Jesus could endure the worst suffering of all—separation from God while dying on the cross. What are some heavenly joys that can encourage you to remain faithful to God, even when your life seems overwhelming?

5. Summarize what the following verses say about whether it's possible for God to forsake Christians:

• Matthew 28:20

• Romans 8:35–39

• Hebrews 13:5

6. Do you agree with the statement: "The Christian's true goal in life is not happiness, but holiness"? Why or why not?

7. The Bible describes hell as a place of eternal punishment. Do you agree with that? If not, what are your beliefs about hell, and why do you not interpret the biblical teaching literally?

8. Name someone you know who is separated from Christ because of unconfessed sin. What might God want you to do for that person?

9. Imagine a friend telling you, "I've asked God for years why my daughter was raped, and He hasn't given me an answer." What would you say to your friend?

A HUMBLING QUESTION:

"Do you have a hardened heart?" (Mark 8:17)

WHEN I WAS NINE YEARS OLD, my parents had a tennis court built in our back yard. I fell in love with it at first sight. For the next thirteen years, I played or practiced tennis several hours a day. Away from the court people would sometimes shake my hand and remark, "This is the hand of a working man." I was always embarrassed to admit my hand was callous from playing tennis rather than chopping wood or wielding a jackhammer. Once I said nothing. Then the man who commented on my hands held them both up and noticed that my left was soft.

A hardened heart is like a callous hand—tough, insensitive, and unresponsive. There is no hiding the thick skin. It immediately catches the attention of others.

The humbling aspect about Jesus' question in Mark 8:17 is that He directed it to His disciples. We tend to think of hardness of heart as something that applies to stubborn unbelievers, such as Pharaoh in Moses' day or the Pharisees who opposed Jesus. But in the present verse, our Lord was cautioning His own followers to guard against this spiritual disease.

Having served as a pastor for more than two decades, I can testify that there is much hardness of heart in churches today. I can also bear firsthand witness that it's easy for me to grow callous to spiritual realities. So examine your heart. Don't assume that Jesus' question is aimed at someone else. Today He asks you to consider seriously whether your heart has become hardened.

FIVE SYMPTOMS OF A HARD HEART

"Do you have a hardened heart?" (Mark 8:17). Here are five symptoms by which you can make a determination. The first is *a lack of love for Christ*. The heart is the seat of love. We say such things as, "I love you with all my heart" and "I give you my heart." The foremost commandment in the Bible tells us to love the Lord our God with all our hearts (Matt. 22:34–40). The members of the first-century Ephesian church experienced a hardening of heart, for Jesus rebuked them with these words: "I have this against you, that you have left your first love" (Rev. 2:4).

When was the last time you told Christ you love Him? When was the last time you shared your love for Christ with someone else? When you do that, does your voice quiver, as if you know the other person won't believe you?

A second sign of a hardened heart is *when spiritual disciplines become routine*. The passion of prayer cools to a sickening lukewarmness. The delight of Bible study becomes a drudgery. You used to look forward to Sundays when you would worship with other believers in the Lord's house. But now your churchgoing is a chore. There was a time when you gave cheerfully and generously to the Lord. You still give, but when you drop your check into the offering plate, a grudging spirit hardens the wall of your heart.

Even listening to the Good News of Christ becomes singsong to the hardhearted person. The gospel used to be beautiful music, but no longer. Now there are stories sweeter to your ear, such as those of your job promotion, last summer's vacation, or your favorite team's most recent victory.

Israel's King David hardened his heart when he refused to confess his sins of adultery and murder. Fortunately for him, when he was confronted, he had enough tenderness left to feel God's conviction and to pray, "Restore to me the joy of Thy salvation" (Ps. 51:12). Could that be a prayer you need to lift to heaven?

A third symptom of a callous heart is *indifference to the lost condition of people apart from Christ*. In times past the mere thought of someone perishing caused you to shudder. But now it doesn't faze you to hear about friends and acquaintances dying in unbelief. You used to be zealous to win the lost to Christ. Now, however, your zeal is lost.

Charlie Peace was a notorious murderer in England. He was finally caught, tried, convicted, and sentenced to die. On the morning of his execution in Armley Jail in Leeds, the chaplain accompanied him to the scaffold from which he would be hanged. While making the way down the corridor, the chaplain was reading verses from the Bible. But his tone of voice and the look on his face were more appropriate to a recitation of names and addresses out of a phone book. The convicted murderer was shocked at the way the chaplain routinely read about death and hell. Turning to the preacher, he said, "If I believed what you and the church say you believe, even if England were covered with broken glass from coast to coast, I would walk over it on hands and knees, if need be, just to save one soul from an eternal hell like that."[1]

Does that statement convict you? If not, you may be falling prey to a fourth symptom of a hardened heart—*the ability to sin with a quiet conscience*. A man confessed to me that he had learned to commit fornication without feeling guilty. The first time he fell into this sin he promised God that if he could only be forgiven, he would flee from this vice the rest of his life. God did forgive him, but the man stumbled a second time. Again he begged the Lord with tears to restore him and vowed that he had learned his lesson. But the tug of temptation kept luring him to his girlfriend's bedroom. Soon he began making excuses for his behavior: "This will be the last time." "I'm only human." "I can't help myself." "It's okay, because we're in love." His heart had become hardened.

Your besetting sin might be lying, cheating, stealing, lust, or outbursts of temper. Whatever it is, if you are able to soften the guilt that God brings home to you at each recurrence, you have begun to petrify your heart.

A man who was wrestling with a conflict in his life sought professional help. "Tell me about your problem," the counselor said.

"When my will power is weak, I do bad things; then my conscience troubles me."

The counselor anticipated his need and replied, "So you want to strengthen your will power."

"No," the man mumbled, "I'd rather weaken my conscience."

Does your heart ever feel that way? If so, it is growing adamant.

A fifth telltale sign of the loss of sensitivity in the heart is *a critical spirit toward God and His work*. In the opening of Mark 3, the Pharisees were finding fault with Jesus for healing a man on the Sabbath. Verse 5 says that this was an evidence of "their hardness of heart."

A spirit-filled couple moved into town and joined the church of which I am pastor. I was delighted to have them. They taught in our Sunday school, sang in our choir, and encouraged other believers. But after a few years, they suddenly stopped coming. I visited their home to find out why. The husband told me, "We tried to stomach the organized church, but we became fed up with the hypocrisy we saw. We just couldn't take it any longer."

I never deny that the church's hypocrisy is a problem; God will hold us accountable for it. But in Jesus' day the most flagrant hypocrites were the critics. When my life falls short of the standards I believe in, I am a hypocrite. There is hypocrisy in all of us. The faultfinders of today are without excuse and may as well fellowship with the rest of us sinners in the church. We need constructive criticism, but a critical attitude toward the work of God reveals an absence of love and a hardened heart.

These five symptoms of a callous heart take place gradually, like a lake that turns to ice overnight or wet cement that solidifies into concrete in a few hours. Charles Swindoll observed:

> No garden "suddenly" overgrows with thorns. No church "suddenly" splits. No building "suddenly" crumbles. No marriage "suddenly" breaks down. No nation "suddenly" becomes a mediocre power. No person "suddenly" becomes base. Slowly, almost imperceptibly, certain things are accepted that once were rejected. Things once considered hurtful are now secretly tolerated. At the outset it appears harmless, perhaps even exciting, but the wedge it brings leaves a gap that grows wider as moral erosion joins hands with spiritual decay. The gap becomes a canyon. That "way which seems right" becomes, in fact, "the way of death."[2]

Thus, hardness of heart is a subtle sin. Like a clock's hands that you can't see move, it creeps up on you and takes you by surprise.

A HARD HEART IS A HEAVY BURDEN

"Do you have a hardened heart?" If so, consider what God's Word says about it. First, the Bible teaches that *a hardened heart is a sin for which we are to blame.* Psalm 95:8 warns, "Do not harden your hearts." That command is repeated three times in the New Testament Book of Hebrews (3:8, 15; 4:7). Those verses teach that we are the ones who harden our hearts.

But doesn't the Bible say that God hardened Pharaoh's heart (Exod. 10:20, 27)? Yes, it does, though in other passages it says that Pharaoh hardened his own heart. Still, when God did the hardening, how can we blame Pharaoh?

That question assumes the Lord forced hardness of heart on Pharaoh. I believe that God was passive in the process. You harden water into ice by pouring it into an ice tray and placing it in the freezer. You actively do these things to it. But to harden bread, all you have to do is leave it alone. Simply neglect to wrap it up in its cellophane bag, and it by its nature will grow stale.

The human heart is like bread. For it to be soft, an outside influence must surround it. That outside influence is the grace of God. Grace, of course, is undeserved favor. Therefore, the heavenly Father is not unfair when He withdraws His gracious influences from our lives. That's what He did with Pharaoh. As a result, the king's heart grew hard. We can say that God hardened Pharaoh's heart by leaving him to his own corruption. Hence, Pharaoh was to blame for his heart of stone, which showed no pity for God's people who were suffering under his tyrannical rule. And still today, every person is morally responsible for the hardness of his or her own heart.

Second, Scripture teaches that *a hardened heart blinds us to God's truth.* The Pharisees once asked Jesus to comment on the Old Testament law of divorce. Our Lord replied, "Because of your hardness of heart, Moses permitted you to divorce your wives; but from the beginning it has not been this way" (Matt. 19:8).

As early as the first marriage in Eden, God made Adam and Eve one flesh (Gen. 2:24). Jesus taught that people should have known that they should not separate what God had joined together (Mark 10:9). Divorce was never His intention. In fact, He even hates it (Mal. 2:16). But the hard hearts of people have blinded them to that truth.

Take another example. Mark 6:52 tells us that the disciples "had not gained any insight from the incident of the loaves, but their heart was hardened." When Jesus fed the five thousand, the disciples should have understood that the miracle pointed beyond itself to Christ as God incarnate. But their hardness of heart darkened their minds.

On another occasion Jesus warned His disciples against "the leaven of the Pharisees and the leaven of Herod" (Mark 8:15). He was speaking about the rapidly spreading influence of their unbelief, hypocrisy, secularism, and worldliness. But the disciples thought He was talking about literal bread. So Jesus rebuked them with these words: "Do you not yet see or understand? Do you have a hardened heart?" (v. 17). Underscore the connection between the disciples' failure to understand and their hardened hearts; the second caused the first.

In Ephesians 4:18, Paul spoke about unbelievers and "the ignorance that is in them due to the hardening of their hearts" (NIV). Note the connection between spiritual ignorance and its cause—hardness of heart.

One evening in our church I was teaching on predestination. It is a difficult doctrine to comprehend, so I was trying to explain it as simply as I could. After the message, a man marched up to me and complained, "I will not serve a God who predestines anything or anyone! If what you taught tonight is true, then we are robots who have no responsibility to accept Christ. I will not believe that!"

This person completely misunderstood me. I had said that God holds us accountable to believe in His Son. The man was unable to hear that, or at least to grasp it, because he had already closed his mind to the biblical truth about predestination. There was no changing him, even though I had stated my case from Scripture. He had hardened his heart.

Do you have difficulty perceiving the truths in God's Word? The problem may have nothing to do with your mind; it could be a matter of your heart. The issue might not be one of intellectual prowess but spiritual callousness. You should prayerfully consider the possibility that you have hardened your heart—the same place from which Christ wants to rule and reign.

A third cause for alarm is that *our spiritual callousness breaks the heart of Jesus.* Consider the Pharisees. Mark 3:5 says that our Lord was "grieved at their hardness of heart." Think about it. Their hard hearts grieved Jesus' heart! He sorrowed over the inability of the Pharisees to repent of their sins. Because they were without feeling for their sin, He was filled with sadness. When they were unable to see Him as the Messiah, He grieved over what they had become. Today Jesus still sorrows over the hardness of heart He sees, not just in the world, but especially in His body, the church.

You Can Soften Your Heart by Using Your Eyes

If you have a hardened heart, go back to Calvary and see Jesus dying on the cross—not just for your sins, but for your hardness of heart. No one who witnessed the death of Christ remained hardhearted. I appeal to Luke 23:48 to support my claim: "And all the multitudes who came together for this spectacle [the crucifixion of Christ], when they observed what had happened, began to return, beating their breasts." Why did they express remorse and anguish in this way? Because their hardened hearts had put Jesus to death, and so they beat their breasts to get to the source of the crime.

This was true of the religious rulers who sneered at Christ, the soldiers who nailed Him to the cross, and the crowds who watched Him die. The text says that "all" of them beat their breasts. They had come to observe a "spectacle." But they left distressed over the execution of an innocent man. The sight of the dying Savior somehow troubled them. We have already seen that hardness of heart causes Jesus to grieve. In the end it made the people who watched His crucifixion grieve, too.

Do you ever mourn your spiritual condition? The Savior pronounced a blessing on people who do (Matt. 5:4). We wouldn't expect sorrow and blessing to go hand in hand, but they do, for sorrow over sin is the first step toward receiving a tender heart. That grief is always the result of looking in faith to the crucified Christ.

The Bible commands us to be tenderhearted (Eph. 4:32). Do you have a hardened heart? If so, confess it to God. Look in faith to the dying Savior, who gave His life to make you new from the inside out. Then expect the heavenly Father to give you His tender heart. Listen to His promise from Ezekiel 36:26: "I will give you a new heart and put a new spirit within you; and I will remove the heart of stone from your flesh and give you a heart of flesh."

Can you trust God for that? If you can, that's a good sign that the Lord has already begun to soften your heart!

Action Steps

Perhaps in all honesty you can say that your heart is tender toward the Lord and sensitive to the touch of His Holy Spirit. Then pray compassionately for people you know who have built spiritual ramparts around their hearts to keep our Lord out. Look for opportunities to share Christ with them. Dare to believe that God has prepared their hearts to hear the gospel. Remind yourself that the Holy Spirit breaks hard hearts by means of soft ones.

At the turn of the twentieth century, C. S. Lewis was raised in the Church of England. But while he was a teenage schoolboy, he became an atheist. Looking back on that time, he testified that he wanted to call his soul his own and to have no one interfere with him. He described his reaction to any mention of the supernatural as that of a drunkard to alcohol—pure nausea. He despised the church and admitted, "I liked clergymen as I liked bears. I had as little wish to be in the Church as in the zoo."

Then God began to melt his hardened heart. He felt "the steady, unrelenting approach of Him whom I so earnestly desired not to meet." But for the first time he examined himself with a seriously practical purpose and "found what appalled me; a zoo of lusts, a bedlam of ambitions, a nursery of fears, a harem of fondled hatreds. My name was legion."

In 1929, Lewis "gave in, and admitted that God was God, and knelt and prayed: perhaps that night, the most dejected and reluctant convert in all England." He had so hardened his heart that even at that moment he was still "kicking, struggling, resentful, and darting his eyes in every direction for a chance to escape."[3] Lewis did not escape. And he who formerly had hardened his heart is known today as one the twentieth century's eloquent defenders of Christian faith. There is always hope for callous unbelievers, so don't grow discouraged in your prayers for people you know whose hearts are petrified against Christ. Neglect of prayer is itself an evidence of hardness of heart.

Jesus is the donor waiting to give you, me, and all the world the heart transplant we desperately need. He goes right to the core of our problem.

Study Guide

1. Summarize what these verses say about the human heart:

   • Genesis 6:5

   • Ecclesiastes 9:3

   • Jeremiah 17:9

   • Matthew 15:18–19

2. Lack of love for Christ is a symptom of a hardened heart. How can you determine whether you truly love Jesus? You can find insight in these verses:

   • John 14:15, 23

   • 1 John 5:3

   • 2 John 6

3. Lack of love for others is also a sign of a spiritually hardened heart. How can you evaluate your love for people?

4. Ephesians 4:18 speaks about "the ignorance" that some hardened people have. Give an example of something that hardhearted people could learn if only their hearts were tender.

5. Mark 3:5 states that Jesus was grieved by hard hearts. Name a sin commonly practiced that must grieve Jesus and that shows people's hardhearted condition. Why did you identify that particular sin?

6. Name someone you know or have heard of who once had a hardened heart but now has a soft heart for Christ. How did God soften that person's heart? If this applies to you, share how God softened your heart.

7. A hardened person tells you, "I know I'm out of fellowship with God, but He understands me and will forgive me, even though I'm not ready to repent." How will you respond?

8. Ephesians 4:32 commands Christians to be "tenderhearted." Each of the passages below shows a sign of a tender heart. What are those signs?

- Mark 12:41–44

- Luke 15:20

- Luke 19:41

- 2 Corinthians 8:5

- Galatians 6:2

- Colossians 3:13

- 1 Thessalonians 1:9

- 1 Peter 1:8

A DECISIVE QUESTION:

"Where is your faith?"
(Luke 8:25)

SOMEONE HAS REMARKED, "To our forefathers, faith was an experience. To our fathers, faith was an inheritance. To us, faith is a convenience. To our children, faith is a nuisance."

How sad this is, especially in light of Scripture's warning that "without faith it is impossible to please God" (Heb. 11:6 NIV). Jesus continually grieved over the lack of faith in His disciples. When they thought their lives were in jeopardy during a violent storm at sea, Jesus rebuked the wind and the surging waves, made the water as smooth as glass, and then asked, "Where is your faith?" (Luke 8:25).

Your answer to that question suggests where you will spend eternity. Jesus implies that you have faith. Everybody does. But where have you placed it?

YOUR FAITH MUST BE ONLY IN CHRIST

What do you believe in? Many would call that an irrelevant question. "All that matters," they claim, "is that you have faith." Take, for example, the group Alcoholics Anonymous. The third of their famous twelve steps of recovery states, "We made a decision to turn our will and our lives over to the care of God as we understood God." The phrase *as we understood God* presumes that faith in any deity will suffice. One publication for the organization says, "We discovered that we did not need to consider another's conception of God. Our own conception, however inadequate, was sufficient to . . . affect a contact with Him. . . .To us, the Realm of Spirit is broad, roomy, all inclusive."[1]

But God is not a smorgasbord. Scripture says that Christ is the only acceptable object of faith (John 3:16, 36). Therefore, to have any efficacy, faith must rest in Him alone.

Donald Malcolm Campbell, a world record holder in boat racing, lost his life on a lake in Scotland when his boat exploded and sank. The only object that surfaced was a stuffed toy animal. Campbell had placed his faith in it as his "good luck charm," but it was an unworthy object, for it was unable to deliver him from the danger he feared.[2]

To spend a twenty-dollar bill, you have to exercise faith in its purchasing power. But the value of the money, not your faith, is the basis of the purchase. If all that mattered were faith, you could buy items with play money.

Christ is the object of our faith. But we don't just believe in Him because we have to believe in *something*. Rather, we know that by trusting in Him we have eternal life. He is the true Savior and Lord of the world.

Scripture states that "God so loved the world, that He gave His only begotten Son, that whoever believes in Him should not perish, but have eternal life" (John 3:16); "He who believes in the Son has eternal life" (v. 36); and "every one who beholds the Son and believes in Him, may have eternal life" (6:40).

When Jesus asked His disciples, "Where is your faith?" (Luke 8:25), He implied that faith could be in the wrong object. You may have faith that God exists, but that doesn't make you a Christian. Your faith may be in some orthodox creed, but a creed is no substitute for Christ. You may have faith that your church is true to the Word of God, but that won't get you into heaven. J. I. Packer commented:

> The historic Roman Catholic idea of faith has been of mere credence and docility. Faith, to Rome, is just belief of what the Roman church teaches. Indeed, Rome actually distinguishes between "explicit" faith (belief of something understood) and "implicit" faith (uncomprehending assent to whatever it may be that the Roman church holds), and says that only the latter—which in reality is just a vote of confidence in the teaching church, and may go along with total ignorance of Christianity— is required of laymen for salvation![3]

The biblical teaching about the nature of saving faith is contrary to what the Roman Catholic church historically has maintained. Scripture declares that only explicit faith in Christ leads to salvation and adoption in God's family. The object of one's faith matters much when it comes to eternal life. You can have the sincerest faith in the world that something or someone other than Christ will save you, but you will be sincerely wrong. The faith of children who believe in Santa Claus can be quite genuine, but it fails to bring them a real Santa Claus. When it comes to our salvation from sin, our faith must be in the one worthy object—Jesus Christ.

YOUR FAITH MUST HAVE FOUR SIDES

Faith in Christ is like a square. To be genuine, it must have four sides. If even one of them is missing, you may well question your standing with God.

First, *faith begins with a willingness to listen to the claims of Christ.* Paul asked, "How shall they believe in Him whom they have not heard?" (Rom. 10:14). The apostle concluded, "So faith comes from hearing, and hearing by the word of Christ" (v. 17).

People are incapable of saving faith who refuse to read Scripture, listen to a gospel sermon, or attend a Bible study. So are people who listen with a closed mind. In the courts of law a verdict for or against a defendant is not delivered until that person has been given a fair hearing. It is the same with a spiritual verdict in favor of Christ. Before people can announce, "I have trusted Christ for salvation," they must say, "I will consider His claims in Scripture."

Second, *faith in Christ involves knowledge.* You have to know the basic facts about the gospel. For example, Jesus is God the Son who came to earth as a man. The heavenly Father sent Him to die on a cross as your substitute. Jesus' shed blood was the ransom price paid to deliver you from sin. His resurrection from the dead validated His payment for sin. If you are unaware of these basic gospel facts, your faith will be in someone other than the Christ of Scripture.

Many people believe wrong things about Christ. They may think He was only a good moral teacher, or that He taught us how to save ourselves, or that because He is loving, He would not allow anyone to go to hell. Faith built on such false notions will result in a bogus salvation.

Here is a test of your basic knowledge concerning Christ and the salvation He offers: Describe the gospel in one sentence. Do you find that difficult? I have always asked candidates I interviewed for pastoral staff positions to do this. I look for an answer along this line: "The gospel is that God sent His Son, Jesus, to die on the cross as the sacrifice for our sins, so that we might have eternal life through faith in Him." To have your faith properly grounded, you need to know those basic facts.

Third, *faith in Christ includes belief.* Many people read the Bible, listen to sermons, and know the gospel, but they don't accept any of it as true. The person with genuine faith says, "I am convinced that Jesus Christ is the only Savior for me." The disciples expressed this kind of faith in John 16:30 when they told Jesus, "We believe that You came from God." Romans 10:9 also stresses our need to believe when it promises, "If you confess with your mouth Jesus as Lord, and believe in your heart that God raised Him from the dead, you shall be saved."

Once you reach this level of belief, or mental assent, don't stop there. Demons believe in the existence of God (James 2:19), yet they oppose Him. This brings us to the fourth element of faith—commitment. *You must commit yourself to the Christ in whom you believe.*

I heard Josh McDowell once say that faith "is when your commitment exceeds your knowledge." When you sit in a chair, you commit your weight to it, even though for all you know it could collapse beneath you. You swallow pills, not because you understand all the pharmaceutical ingredients in them, but because you have confidence in the physician who wrote the prescription. Your commitment to him or her exceeds your knowledge of medicine. When you drive a car, its brakes might not be operating properly. But even before you've tested the brake pedal, you commit yourself by placing your foot on the accelerator. Your commitment to the car exceeds your knowledge of its mechanical condition. That's the commitment aspect of faith.

The necessity of commitment in faith is one of the lessons in Jesus' parable of the soils (Matt. 13:1–23). It illustrates four kinds of hearts: those that are like a path, rocky soil, thorns, and good soil. All four soils received the seed of God's Word, but only one bore fruit. We may think that the path, rocky soil, and thorns represent immature believers. But if that were true, Jesus would be teaching that everyone who hears God's Word becomes converted. Obviously, that isn't the case. The three poor soils stand for people who show some indications of faith. We saw earlier that faith begins with receptivity. The path, rocky soil, and thorns received the seed of God's Word, but that was all. They symbolize people who never commit themselves to Christ and thus remain spiritually lost.

In the Gospel of John, the Greek nouns for "faith" and "belief" never occur. But the Greek verb for "believe" is found ninety-eight times. John is telling us that faith is active, not passive. It doesn't just sit idle in the brain; it moves on to commitment.

Again, when the New Testament speaks about believing in Christ, it usually states the concept in the form of "believing *into* Christ." John 3:16, for example, literally reads in the Greek, "For God so loved the world, that He gave His only begotten Son, that whoever believes *into* Him will not perish, but have eternal life." We learn from this that faith moves people to leave their sinful self behind and be spiritually united to Christ.

I once heard of a ship's captain whose young son climbed the mast while out at sea. Once up, he was too frightened to climb down. So the father shouted up to him, "The next time the ship lurches, drop into the sea!" The ship lurched several times, but the boy continued to hold on for dear life. His hands were tiring rapidly, however, and he knew that if he didn't commit himself to obeying his father, he would soon fall to the deck. Finally in desperation the boy dropped into the water while the ship was leaning to its side. His father scooped him out, and he was rescued.

Like that boy, we have no hope of salvation except in committing ourselves by faith to Christ. The gospel tells us to fall into His saving arms, for only in Him will we be safe.

Martin Luther expressed such commitment when he testified, "I would run into Jesus' arms even if He had a drawn sword in His hand." Instead of a drawn sword, our Lord has wounds in His hands. They speak to us and say, "I love you! I was crucified for you!"

How easy it is to trust a Savior like that!

Al Munger tells the following story about driving down a narrow, two-lane, twisting road through the hills toward Mazatlan, Mexico:

> Our friends, Betty and Joe, had just piloted their motor home around a big truck that was coughing diesel smoke. Now it was our turn to pass this monster. A dozen impatient drivers were behind us. CURVA PELIGROSA (Dangerous Curve) the sign warned. We could only see about one hundred and fifty feet ahead before the road disappeared around the mountain, but I decided to go for it. Shifting into second gear, I put the pedal to the floor and we started around the truck. The drivers behind us must have thought we were crazy. An oncoming bus or truck would scatter us all over the landscape. But they didn't know that just seconds before we started to pass, Betty had called us on the CB radio saying, "The road ahead is clear for half a mile." The move that appeared suicidal was safe because our friends could see the road ahead and knew there were no cars coming. I chose to believe Betty. I knew she wouldn't lie to me.[4]

That's what the commitment level of faith in Christ is all about. It's trusting in the promises of God's Word enough to act on them, even when the road ahead looks scary and you can't see where it leads. Jesus said that His sheep not only hear His voice but also follow Him (John 10:27). Like the car that followed the motor home around the bend of a narrow road because its driver heard the voice of assurance from up ahead, so a believer trusts Jesus enough to follow Him—and not just through the door of salvation on the day of conversion, but also through grief, affliction, persecution, trials, and death itself.

Trusting in Christ to lead us around every spiritual bend in our road of life reminds me of Louisa Stead's hymn:

> *'Tis so sweet to trust in Jesus,*
> *Just to take Him at His word,*
> *Just to rest upon His promise,*
> *Just to know, "Thus saith the Lord."*
> *Jesus, Jesus, how I trust Him!*
> *How I've proved Him o'er and o'er!*
> *Jesus, Jesus, precious Jesus!*
> *O for grace to trust Him more!*[5]

We can see all four elements of faith illustrated in a marriage relationship. At first the man and woman have to show some receptivity to each other. He must be willing to ask her out on a date, and she must accept his invitation. Once this stage is passed, the element of knowledge comes into play. The couple learn about one another—their likes, their dislikes, their personality makeups, and the things they believe in. After that they enter the level of belief. The man and woman become convinced that they are right for each other. They believe God has brought them together and wants them to spend the rest of their lives united in marriage. Finally, they commit themselves to each other by reciting marriage vows of fidelity to one another, to which God and the wedding guests are witnesses. Thus, from beginning to end, a good marriage is built on the foundation of faith.

ONLY THROUGH FAITH CAN YOU PLEASE GOD

Hebrews 11:6 tells us that without faith it is impossible to please God. The other side of that truth is found in 1 Thessalonians 2:15, which says that those who have no faith in Christ do not please God. There are three reasons we must exercise faith in Christ.

First, *only faith in Christ produces good works God can accept.* The Bible speaks about "your work produced by faith" (1 Thess. 1:3 NIV). Unless faith in Christ is the mainspring of our good works, they are unacceptable to God.

Some time ago I found a Canadian dime in my possession. I tried to use it to pay for groceries, but the clerk refused to accept it. Later I attempted to use it to pay for gasoline, but again it was rejected. I've even been warned by soft drink and newspaper machines, "Do not use

Canadian coins." Of course, we don't blame the Canadians for using their coins, but in America—which is where I live—they frequently are unacceptable.

In the same way, though lack of faith in Christ can lead to good works that impress people, they do not please God. He operates on a divine system, not a human one. Unless we start with faith in Christ, even our religious works are nothing more than camouflaged sins.

Second, *faith in Christ is vital for us because it reveals itself by loving others.* Galatians 5:6 tells us that "in Christ Jesus neither circumcision nor uncircumcision means anything, but faith working through love." We can paraphrase that verse as follows: "In Christianity, rituals mean nothing, but faith in Christ means everything, for it prompts us to love others."

Does your faith work? Does it express itself in love to the Father and to His Son, Jesus? Do you love your Christian brothers and sisters? How about those who are spiritually lost? In His Sermon on the Mount, Jesus said, "Love your enemies" (Matt. 5:44). If you honestly can't say you do that, your faith is not working as it should. Possibly there's no authentic faith in your heart at all.

The concept of faith working through love is sometimes passed over in the euphoria of evangelism. We explain to nonbelievers that they are spiritually lost and in need of Christ. We lead them in the sinner's prayer, in which they confess their sins to God and put their trust in Christ as their Savior. Then we assure them that because they prayed the right words, they are born again. Usually they are. But sometimes this experience of "faith" is a matter only of the head and not of the heart. The reason so many people who have recited the sinner's prayer continue to live in rebellion against Christ is that they still don't love Him. And when love is absent, faith is dead.

Third, *you must have faith in Christ, for in His sacrifice alone is the means of salvation.* "For by grace you have been saved through faith" (Eph. 2:8). Eternal issues are decided in this life on the basis of your faith or your lack of it. Only if you "believe in the name of the Son of God" can "you have eternal life" (1 John 5:13).

This information gives us a glimpse into the earnestness of Jesus when He asked His disciples, "Where is your faith?" (Luke 8:25). What was true of the Twelve is still true of you. If your faith is in the wrong place, it will cost you your soul. Therefore, the key question is not, "Do you have faith?" but rather, "On what is your faith set?" Is it in your baptism? Are you trusting in church membership, good works, or some notion about God that is contrary to Scripture? Such faith will not only fail to get you into heaven; it will make you the laughingstock of hell.

Action Steps

Let me suggest two ways you can respond to this crucial question from Luke 8:25. First, ask God to reveal to you where you have placed your ultimate trust. Maybe you've been counting on your moral life to make you right with God. Or perhaps your faith has been in a god who is unlike the biblical one—a god who doesn't punish sin, or one who will let you into heaven even if you neglect to accept His Son as your Savior.

Andrew Jackson began his first term as President of the United States in 1829. That year a man named George Wilson was convicted of murder and sentenced to death. Jackson knew something about the case and was convinced of Wilson's innocence, so he granted the condemned man a presidential pardon. But to the President's surprise, Wilson not only refused it but argued that his rejection of the pardon rendered it null and void.

The state attorney of Pennsylvania, where Wilson was imprisoned, reported back that the law was silent on this point. No one had ever turned down a pardon. The case found its way up to the United States Supreme Court. Chief Justice John Marshall ultimately wrote, "A pardon is just a piece of paper unless it is accepted by the person implicated. If he refuses the pardon, it is not a pardon. George Wilson must hang." A few months later he did.[6]

If your faith doesn't prompt you to accept God's free gift of eternal life in the person of His Son, then on the day of judgment, you will begin to suffer eternal loss in hell. It's that simple and clear (see Rev. 20:11–15).

Where is your faith? Has it fixed itself on Christ in complete trust? In her autobiographical hymn, Lidie Edmunds spoke of the joy of a personal faith fixed on the right object:

> *My faith has found a resting place,*
> *Not in a man-made creed;*
> *I trust the ever-living One,*
> *That He for me will plead.*
> *I need no other argument,*
> *I need no other plea;*
> *It is enough that Jesus died*
> *And that He died for me.*[7]

Once you've planted your faith in Christ, you're ready to take the second step. Ask God how He wants you to show your faith. We saw from Galatians 5:6 that faith works through love. What loving act does God want you to do as an exercise of your faith? He may be calling you to serve cheerfully in the children's ministry of your church. He may be asking you to start giving a responsible financial offering on a regular basis. It could be a task as simple as visiting a lonely person in a convalescent hospital. However you practice faith in Christ, it will bring God's grace to others and His assurance to you. Then faith will no longer be a convenience or a nuisance. It will be your life.

Study Guide

1. Define faith in your own words.

2. Hebrews 11:6 says, "Without faith it is impossible to please God" (NIV). Why do you think faith pleases God?

3. Imagine that a professing Christian says to you, "Jews, Muslims, Buddhists, Hindus, and Christians—we all believe in the same God. The difference is only in the name." How will you respond?

4. Summarize what the following verses teach about faith in Christ:

   • John 3:18

   • John 3:36

   • Acts 16:31

   • Romans 10:9–10

5. What do these verses teach about unbelief?

    • Mark 6:6

    • Mark 9:24

    • Mark 16:14

    • Hebrews 3:12

6. Hebrews 11 is the great chapter on faith. Read Hebrews 11:36–40. What important lesson does this passage teach you about living by faith? Does that lesson surprise you? Why or why not?

7. Read Luke 7:1–9, in which Jesus marveled at a centurion's faith. What was so marvelous about this man's faith?

8. Read Matthew 4:5–7. Satan tempted Jesus to jump off the pinnacle of the Jerusalem temple to display His faith. After all, didn't Psalm 91:11–12 state that angels would prevent the righteous from striking their foot on a stone? Why did Jesus refuse to jump? What was deceptive about the temptation?

9. Galatians 5:6 speaks about "faith working through love." Share a personal experience when your faith in Christ "worked." What was the result?

10. Besides Christ and His finished work on the cross, what object of faith have you been tempted to trust in for salvation?

A DOCTRINAL QUESTION:

"What is written in the Law?"
(Luke 10:26)

ANDREW BONAR USED TO TELL a story about a Christian who died and went to heaven. As he strolled around the streets of gold, he came upon a group of authors of biblical books: Isaiah, Ezekiel, and Obadiah. The Christian introduced himself to each one and exchanged handshakes. "It's a privilege to meet you," he said. "I've heard so much about each of you." Isaiah then asked, "What did you think about my book?"

With an embarrassed look on his face, the Christian answered, "I'm sorry, but I never got around to reading it."

Obadiah broke the tension by saying, "Isaiah is rather long-winded with his sixty-six chapters. But my book has only one chapter. Surely you read it. What did you think about it?"

Again the Christian blushed and admitted that he had not read it. Then, in an attempt to gain some understanding, he said, "Obadiah. . . . Let's see. . . . Is that in the Old or New Testament?"

Are you headed for the same potential embarrassment? In Luke 10, a scribe asked Jesus what he had to do to inherit eternal life (v. 25), and our Lord countered with a question of His own: "What is written in the Law?" (v. 26). Jesus wanted this expert in the Mosaic law to discover the answer to his own question through his knowledge of the Old Testament. And the scribe did! After listening to his succinct answer, Jesus told him he had responded correctly (vv. 27–28).

Today there are many false notions about the Old Testament's message. Some say it was written to teach us to earn our salvation by working for it. Others claim it presents a God who is drastically different from the God of the New Testament. Still others assert that the Old Testament applies only to the Jew and not to the Christian. Some Christians completely discard the Old Testament, as if the New Testament renders it unnecessary.

So what should we believe about the Old Testament and the Mosaic law? A survey of the New Testament can help clarify things for us. It gives five answers to Jesus' question, "What is written in the Law?"

THE LAW SHOWS US OUR SIN

Three verses in Paul's letter to the Romans stress this purpose of the law. The first, Romans 3:20, informs us that "through the Law comes the knowledge of sin." You might ask, "Do people have to be told that they are sinful? Isn't that obvious to them?" No! Amazingly enough, if the Bible did not tell us that we are sinners, we would not know it. Sometimes people with cancer feel fine and are unaware of their disease. A physician has to inform them. In a similar way, the law of God is the "physician" that introduces us to our spiritual disease called "sin."

Take, for example, the Ten Commandments, which form the essence of God's moral law. The commandment, "You shall not steal" (Exod. 20:15), reminds you of times when you might have filched something. Even if you are not a common thief, you might be haunted by memories of snitching cookies out of your mother's cookie jar, or of taking candy from a store, or of neglecting to repay money you "borrowed" from a friend.

The law is like a mirror that reflects the perfect righteousness of God and our own sinfulness and shortcomings (James 1:23–25). Imagine a man getting up in the morning and looking at his reflection in the mirror. He sees whiskers, disheveled hair, yellow teeth, and a dirty smudge on his face. The mirror lets him know what he needs to do to make himself look right. But no mirror ever shaved a man's beard, combed his hair, brushed his teeth, or scrubbed his face.

And so it is with the law of God. When we look into it, we see our spiritual blemishes. It reflects our sins of jealousy, anger, lying, gossip, unbelief, and lovelessness (to name a few). We still have to repent of our sins and trust in Christ for salvation. Nevertheless, without the spiritual "mirror" of the law, we would not know that we had offended our holy God.

Romans 5:20 teaches a similar lesson: "The Law came in that the transgression might increase." God's law is like a magnifying glass that you use to inspect a garment. The magnifying glass does not create spots on the garment, but it does make them appear larger, and thus it helps you to see the stains in the fabric. The lens also reveals spots you could not see with the unaided eye.

Like that magnifying glass, the Old Testament law increases our aware-
ness of the rampant presence of sin in our lives. When we look through
the powerful "lens" of the law, we see more clearly the full heinousness
of our sin. The law also shows how utterly contemptible our sin is against
the backdrop of God's holiness.

A third verse sheds even more light on this subject. In Romans 7:7,
Paul spoke for us all when he testified, "I would not have come to know
sin except through the Law; for I would not have known about coveting
if the Law had not said, 'You shall not covet.'" The prohibition against
covetousness is the last of the Ten Commandments and can be applied
to all nine of the previous commandments. It implies that all of God's
laws can be violated not just in our outward acts but also in our hearts.

Though the law itself is not sinful (see 7:12), it brings into the open
the power of sin. Once sin is aroused in us, we long to participate in its
despicable acts (see vv. 8–11). A woman once objected to the reading of
the Ten Commandments in church because "they put so many ideas into
people's minds." That's exactly right!

A man bought a new refrigerator and wanted to get rid of his old, broken one. But it would cost him money to have someone haul it away and
dispose of it. So he hung a sign on his useless refrigerator that read, "FOR
SALE: $50." Then he rolled it out to the sidewalk in front of his house.
The next morning the refrigerator was gone! It was as if his sign had
said, "You shall not steal." Which is exactly why someone did.

That is what Paul was getting at when he talked about the law arous-
ing sin within us. Sin uses the specific requirements of the law as a base
of operation from which to launch its evil work. When our rebellious
nature is confronted by God's law, we find that the forbidden is more
attractive. It is not that the sinful act is inherently enticing, but it attracts
by giving us an opportunity to assert our self-will. For example, when
Adam and Eve ate the forbidden fruit in the garden, they were claiming
their independence from God.

When Napoleon's troops approached the Alps, he asked his scouts,
"Is it possible to get the whole army over the top?"

"Barely possible," was the reply. And so they started out. Thousands
perished in the attempt. What if the Alps had been twice as high?
Napoleon's counselors would have told him there was no chance of getting over, and he never would have attempted a climb that took countless lives.

The spiritual intent of God's law is like the Alps on top of the Alps.
When we read the commandment "You shall not murder" (Exod.
20:13), we might confidently assert, "I can obey that!" But then Jesus
declared that anyone who is angry with someone is guilty of murder in
God's eyes (Matt. 5:21–22). When we hear the command, "You shall

not commit adultery" (Exod. 20:14), we might boast, "I can stay away from that!" But then Jesus equated adultery with lust in the heart (Matt. 5:27–28). Now we are infinitely more challenged by the presence and power of sin.

Jesus was not adding anything new to the law; the divine intent was there all along, especially in the commandment against coveting. The religious leaders of Israel had conveniently overlooked this truth for centuries, and our Lord reminded them of it. He was teaching them that keeping the law is not just a matter of outward actions but also of inward attitudes.

When we grasp that truth, the law seems infinitely more difficult to obey. Keeping its commandments is like trying to move an army over the Alps when the mountains are thousands of miles high. This helps us to see how thoroughly sinful we really are and how utterly incapable we are of resisting sin and heeding the law.

THE LAW MAKES US DESPAIR OF SAVING OURSELVES

Once we realize our sinful condition, our human nature says, "I must solve this problem; I will make myself better!" Then we try desperately to please God and save ourselves. We may even gain a degree of control over our sins. But of course we all have our individual weaknesses. For you it may be outbursts of temper, profanity, lust, gluttony, or something else. You begin to think that, if only you could conquer that one besetting sin, you would be spiritually whole.

That's where God's law comes in. It warns us that "whoever keeps the whole law and yet stumbles in one point, he has become guilty of all" (James 2:10). God's law is not like an exam at school, on which you can miss a few questions and still receive an *A* grade. It is like a tire on a car. If a nail punctures any part of it, the whole tire goes flat.

Or consider a football team. If one player is offside, the whole team is penalized. However good the other players might be, they will all suffer loss if that one person continues to encroach into forbidden territory. Your moral life is made up of many teammates on the scrimmage line. Most of the moral elements may be under near-perfect control, but as long as there is one flaw, your moral being is completely out of sorts with God.

What is written in the law? Its message declares, "You cannot solve your sin problem!" If it were not for that message, we would become tangled in a net of self-righteousness. Hence, the kindness of God working through His law brings us to the point of realizing our need for grace in Christ (Gal. 3:24).

THE LAW ILLUSTRATES THE GOSPEL

Throughout the Old Testament we see pictures of Christ and His work on the cross. The many lambs slain on sacrificial altars typify Jesus, who was sacrificed for our sins. For example, in Genesis 22, Abraham was about to offer his son Isaac as a human sacrifice in obedience to God's command. But at the last moment the Lord stopped Abraham and showed him a ram that could take Isaac's place. That ram represents Jesus, our Substitute. He accepted the punishment we deserved when God's wrath was unleashed on Him at Calvary.

The primary sacrifice in the Old Testament was the Passover lamb (Exod. 12). God told the Israelites to take a spotless lamb, kill it, and smear its blood on the tops and sides of their doorposts. That night an angel killed the firstborn in every home in which there was no blood on the doorposts. Those who had the blood in place were passed over by the judgment. This explains the name "Passover." That Passover lamb was a preview of Jesus. When by faith we trust in His shed blood to save us from our sins, God passes over us. He spares us from the judgment we rightly deserve because His Son was judged in our place.

Psalm 22 and Isaiah 53 prophesy of the crucifixion of Christ. So does the brass snake that Moses lifted up on a pole in obedience to God, so that all who looked to it would be healed of their snake bites (Num. 21:5–9; John 3:14–15). Notice that the cure was just like the problem. A look to the brass snake healed people of the poison of the literal snakes. In the same way, the crucified Christ became sin for us that through faith in Him we might be healed of the sin in our hearts. As Paul explained in 2 Corinthians 5:21, God "made Him who knew no sin to be sin on our behalf, that we might become the righteousness of God in Him."

When Jesus walked with the two disciples on the road to Emmaus, "beginning with Moses and with all the prophets, He explained to them the things concerning Himself in all the Scriptures" (Luke 24:27). Later that day He spoke to a larger group of disciples about "all things which are written about Me in the Law of Moses and the Prophets and the Psalms" (v. 44).

Many Christians falsely assume that only the New Testament preaches salvation through faith in Christ. But if that were true, there would be two gospels—one in the Old Testament and one in the New. Yet the gospel that we see revealed in the New Testament is the same one that believers looked forward to in the Old Testament. In this regard, the law prepares us for Christ with its many illustrations of our need for a Savior. C. H. Spurgeon wrote:

I do not believe that any man can preach the gospel who does not preach the law. The law is the needle, and you cannot draw the silken thread of the gospel through a man's heart unless you first send the needle of the law to make way for it. If men do not understand the law, they will not feel that they are sinners. And if they are not consciously sinners, they will never value the sin offering. There is no healing a man till the law has wounded him, no making him alive till the law has slain him.[1]

THE LAW DRIVES US TO CHRIST

Paul wrote that the law, as expressed in the Old Testament, "shut up all men under sin, that the promise by faith in Jesus Christ might be given to those who believe" (Gal. 3:22). Like a judge, God's law declares us to be prisoners of sin. Satan may whisper in our hearts that sin brings freedom, but in reality it only enslaves us.

Verse 23 pictures the law as a jailer of guilty, condemned prisoners awaiting divine judgment. We were in protective custody (so to speak) until we could put our faith in Christ. Though in our unsaved condition we are enslaved to sin, there is a door of escape. Jesus is the door of escape, and faith is the arm that reaches out and opens the door.

Verse 24 says, "Therefore the Law has become our tutor to lead us to Christ, that we may be justified by faith." The Greek noun rendered "tutor" does not mean a teacher but an attendant, custodian, or guardian. In wealthy Greek and Roman families this was a hired person whose responsibility was to train, correct, and discipline a child.[2]

If the child stretched the truth, the tutor would speak up and say, "That's a lie!" If the child was about to steal something, the tutor would possibly slap his hands. If the child wanted to go some place where he did not belong, the tutor most likely would warn, "Stay away from there!" In a similar manner, God's law is our guardian and guide to point us to Christ. The law also makes us aware of our need for redemption and spiritual cleansing. It condemns our depraved state so that we will turn to Jesus in faith as our only hope of eternal rescue.

THE LAW TEACHES US TO LOVE

The scribe to whom Jesus originally asked the question, "What is written in the Law?" (Luke 10:26), gave this answer: "You shall love the LORD your God with all your heart, and with all your soul, and with all your strength, and with all your mind; and your neighbor as yourself" (v. 27). Hearing that, Jesus replied, "You have answered correctly" (v. 28).

The Jews counted 613 commands in the law of Moses—248 positives and 365 negatives. We might think that it would be impossible to summarize all those dos and don'ts in one command, but this scribe did just that. When you digest the entire Old Testament law, the result is the word *love*. Love God with everything you've got, and love your neighbor as yourself. Paul agreed when he wrote that love is the fulfillment of the law (Rom. 13:10).

Look again at the Ten Commandments. The first four teach us to love God with all our being. When we do that, we will have no other gods before Him, we will not worship idols, we will not take His name in vain, and we will remember to set aside a day each week to worship Him.

The last six commandments teach us to love our neighbor as ourselves. Love compels us to honor our fathers and mothers. If we love our neighbor, we will certainly not murder or even hate. Love for our neighbor will prevent us from committing adultery with our neighbor's spouse. You avoid stealing from those you love. Nor do you tell lies to or about them. You don't even begrudge your neighbor anything good, for there is no room for coveting in a heart that is already filled with love. And so it is that love for God and for other people is the essence of the law.

Love is the natural outcome of the law. We love God because His law reveals our sin and thus awakens us to our lost condition. We love God for using His law to make us despair of saving ourselves, for that delivers us from self-righteousness. We love God for illustrating in His law the gospel of Christ, for the law sheds much needed light on New Testament doctrine. We love God for using His law to drive us to Christ, for apart from Him there is no salvation. And we love others, because either they are our brothers and sisters in Christ, or they have the same need to know Him that we have.

Action Steps

We Christians tend to spend most all our Bible-reading time in the New Testament, don't we? Have you ever read the Old Testament from beginning to end? When you arrive in heaven, will you be embarrassed to meet prophets like Isaiah and Obadiah, because you neglected to read their books?

One positive way to respond to Jesus' question is to study all of Scripture systematically. Set aside a time each day to listen to the voice of God in His Word. At the rate of fifteen minutes a day, most people can read the entire Bible in less than a year. It takes discipline, but every Christian can feast on the riches of Scripture daily throughout the year. Those who are blind or unable to read can listen to it on audio cassettes.

Lack of commitment is the only thing that prevents a believer from knowing what is written in God's Word.

Do you know what is written in the Law? Perhaps your honest answer to Jesus' question is, "I don't know, Lord. I've never read it." If so, then commit yourself to a prayerful and daily study through all of Scripture.

But don't stop there. Our purpose in reading the Bible is not merely to feed ourselves, but to feed others. Jesus has entrusted us with the responsibility of sharing His good news with others who are unaware of their lost condition. For starters, how about reading Scripture to your own children? My wife and I have done that most every evening for many years, and God has blessed our three children with unashamed faith in Christ and love for Him. There are people all around you who will not read the Bible, but they will listen to you. Any knowledge they are going to receive from God's Word must come from your mouth.

What is written in the Law? A divine message of love, forgiveness, and salvation in Jesus Christ that is meant for all humankind.

Study Guide

1. What is your greatest hesitation or fear when it comes to reading the Old Testament?

2. Which book in the Old Testament do you most enjoy reading and why?

3. This chapter discussed five answers to the question, "What is written in the Law?" Since all five answers apply to the entire Bible, why can't we just read the New Testament?

4. Share an experience when you realized your guilt, either as a nonbeliever or as a Christian. What part, if any, did Scripture play in bringing you to this realization?

5. Some Old Testament laws and practices no longer apply to the Christian, while others do. How do you know which must be obeyed? Give an example of an Old Testament law or practice that Christians need not follow today.

6. Romans 5:20 says that God's law was introduced in order to increase wrongdoing. Someone might read that and complain, "My sin is all God's fault! If He had simply left me without His law, I would not be such an awful sinner!" How would you answer that complaint? Refer to the discussion above and to the related passages from Romans.

7. Many have said that the God of the Old Testament is wrathful, while the God of the New Testament is loving. Draw a specific comparison from both testaments to show that God is the same.

8. Read 2 Timothy 3:16–17. Describe what the inspiration of Scrip-
    ture means.

9. According to each passage below, what is the Word of God able
    to do for you?

    • Psalm 119:105

    • Isaiah 55:10–11

    • John 15:3

    • Romans 10:17

    • 2 Timothy 3:16–17

    • Hebrews 4:12

    • 1 Peter 1:23

    • 1 Peter 2:2

6

AN INTRIGUING QUESTION:

"Do you suppose that these Galileans were greater sinners than all other Galileans, because they suffered this fate?"
(Luke 13:2)

IT WAS JANUARY 28, 1986. Six American astronauts, including a woman civilian elementary school teacher, climbed aboard the Challenger space shuttle. Just seconds into its flight disaster struck, and all six astronauts perished in a ball of fire. In the hours that followed, horrified television watchers witnessed the explosion dozens of times before their television sets. Does the ghastly death of those astronauts suggest that they were secretly more wicked than other scientists, pilots, or school teachers?

Or consider what happened on December 21, 1988. Pan American flight 103 was about to cross the Atlantic Ocean from Europe to the United States. But high over Scotland, a bomb exploded in the cargo section of the plane. No one on board survived the incident. Body parts were scattered for miles around the city of Lockerbe. The singing group *The Temptations* had been booked on flight 103 but canceled at the last minute to do one more concert in Europe. Why were *The Temptations* spared? Were they better than other people? Had they contributed more to the happiness of humankind, or was their music needed more?

What about a man who contracts the HIV virus while committing adultery against his wife, then puts her life in jeopardy before he learns that he has the fatal disease? Eventually the truth is revealed, and his wife is tested. No, she does not have the virus. Did God spare her because she was the innocent victim, or because she was exposed while showing sincere love to her unfaithful husband?

Such scenarios and questions are not new. The oldest book in the Bible, Job, tackled such issues about suffering. In Luke 13:1–5, Jesus Himself broached the subject twice.

YOU CAN'T JUDGE SINNERS BY THEIR SUFFERING

Luke 13:1–5 begins with news of an outrageous act of murder: "Now on the same occasion there were some present who reported to [Jesus] about the Galileans, whose blood Pilate had mingled with their sacrifices" (v. 1). Galileans occupied the northernmost of Palestine's three provinces. The people mentioned in this verse had journeyed south to Jerusalem for a Jewish festival. While making an offering in obedience to the law of Moses, the Galilean Jews were butchered after the always fearful Pilate mistakenly heard that trouble was starting and sent in his soldiers. The reporters of this news added the grisly detail that the altars of sacrifice flowed with the blood of both the offerings and the worshipers.

This incident harmonizes with two secular sources—Josephus and Philo—both contemporaries of Pilate. Philo called him "inflexible, merciless, and obstinate" and spoke about his acts of cruelty and his tendency to punish people mercilessly without a fair trial. Josephus wrote that Pilate slaughtered three thousand Jews and filled the temple with their corpses. On another occasion, he wreaked the same atrocity on two thousand Jews.[1]

Pilate's bloodthirsty act mentioned in Luke 13:1 was naturally the talk of the town, and the crowd wanted to know what Jesus thought about it. Instead of answering their question, He asked one of His own: "Do you suppose that these Galileans were greater sinners than all other Galileans because they suffered this fate?" (v. 2). At first glance it appeared that the people reported Pilate's massacre to evoke Jesus' condemnation of him. But Christ's response highlights a side issue, because Jews tended to believe that good fortune automatically came to the righteous, and suffering was a sign of sin.

Undoubtedly, the people with Jesus that day were Judeans, southerners who often stereotyped the Galileans as immoral and crude. When Nathanael first learned that Jesus hailed from Nazareth in Galilee, he asked incredulously, "Can any good thing come out of Nazareth?" (John 1:46). We can understand, therefore, the Jews in Luke 13:1 to be saying, "Those Galileans whose blood Pilate mingled with their sacrifices must have been the scum of the earth to deserve such a fate!"

Verse 3 tells us Christ's reply: "I tell you, no, but, unless you repent, you will all likewise perish." Jesus was saying that people who suffer more than others are not necessarily greater sinners. If they were, we could measure a person's spirituality by the amount of comfort he or she enjoys. In Jesus' mind it wasn't beyond the realm of possibility that some of the best people in Israel died at Pilate's hands.

Our Lord warned His listeners not to speculate about those who were murdered, but rather to inspect their own lives. If they didn't repent, they would perish. While He wasn't speaking just of Roman swords, Jesus' warning was literally fulfilled in the year 70, when the people of Judea were massacred by Roman soldiers. Because they failed to repent of their sins and turn to Christ in faith, they experienced an atrocity more hideous than the one they had described.

Jesus knew that His warning wouldn't penetrate the thick skulls of His listeners easily, so another illustration reinforced it: "Or do you suppose that those eighteen on whom the tower in Siloam fell and killed them, were worse culprits than all the men who live in Jerusalem?" (v. 4).

Pilate's slaughter of the Galileans was a heartless act, but the fall of the tower of Siloam was evidently an accident. These victims were Judeans, not Galileans. Jesus was implying, "If you think an unusual death is a sign of unusual sin, you can't point the finger of accusation at Galileans only. Some of your own neighbors died in the catastrophe of Siloam's tower. Were they guilty of greater sin than were others who survived?"

In the case of the Galileans, Jesus asked whether they were greater "sinners" than all other Galileans (v. 2). But in verse 4, He used the Greek noun rendered "culprits." The Greek literally means "debtors."[2] This teaches us that people owe God their obedience. Responding positively to Jesus and His gospel are not options for us. Throughout the New Testament God doesn't ask or invite us to believe; He commands us.

Jesus answered His second question in almost exactly the same words as He answered His first: "I tell you, no, but, unless you repent, you will all likewise perish" (v. 5). In verse 3, the adverb "likewise" could refer to the way these people would die. Just as the Galileans had their blood mingled with their sacrifices, the Jews would suffer a similar fate in the overthrow of Jerusalem in A.D. 70.

But we could take the word "likewise" in verse 5 to mean, "you will perish quickly and without warning." The tower crushed those eighteen people to death when they least expected it. And in a similar way, unrepentant people will perish instantly. They may pass away quietly in their beds with their families surrounding them, but from the moment of their last breath, they are hopelessly lost.

A Sinful World Will Suffer

Look again at Jesus' two questions. In Luke 13:2, He did not ask, "Do you suppose that these Galileans were sinners because they suffered this fate?" Instead, He spoke about them as being "*greater* sinners." Again in verse 4 He did not ask, "Do you suppose those eighteen on whom the tower in Siloam fell were culprits before God?" Instead, His real question was, "Were they *worse* culprits than others?"

If there were no sin in this world, there would be no tragic deaths, for death is the consequence of sin in the human race (see Gen. 2:17; 3:17–19; Rom. 5:12; 6:23). If Jesus' chief lesson had been that the victims of Pilate's murder and of the accident in Siloam were blameless, His warning, "unless you repent, you will all likewise perish," would have fallen flat. His point was that the deaths of these people did not prove they were *greater* sinners than others who continued to live.

Years ago a drunk driver attempted to pass a car on a two-lane road at a blind corner. He smashed head-on into a car filled with men from our church, who were returning from a Christian conference. One of our men was in a coma for a month. He made a partial recovery but lost his sight as a result of the accident. Then he lost his job. Later his wife, who was unable to deal with the crisis, divorced him and married another man. Today this man continues to be a dear servant of the Lord, just as he was before. He carries no bitterness in his heart toward the drunk motorist, his former wife, or the Lord.

How could something that tragic happen to someone so wonderful? It's because we live in a sinful world. The sin of one man who drove drunk robbed another man of his job, his sight, and his wife. Was the victim innocent? Yes and no. He didn't deserve this experience any more than did the others in that car who escaped harm, but neither was he perfect. He, like everyone else, needed a Savior. And happily, he had trusted in Christ for redemption. This man proved that his faith was genuine by remaining loyal to Christ despite the tragedy he experienced.

Self-Righteous People Judge Those Who Suffer

The people who died at the order of Pilate and under the tower in Siloam were sinners, no more and no less than anyone else as far as we know. No one who has fallen short of the glory of God has a right to stand in judgment against people who suffer misfortune.

Job's so-called friends didn't understand that. They witnessed his extraordinary suffering and presumed that it was proof of secret sin in his life. Eliphaz spoke for all three when he asked Job, "Is it because you are good that [God] is punishing you? Not at all! It is because of your wickedness! Your sins are endless!" (Job 22:4–5 LB). Eliphaz went on to speculate that Job greedily refused to loan money to needy friends, withheld water from the thirsty and bread from the starving, turned his back on widows, and broke the arms of orphans (vv. 6–9).

One day Jesus and His disciples met a man who had been blind from birth. The disciples asked, "Rabbi, who sinned, this man or his parents, that he should be born blind?" (John 9:2). They jumped to the incorrect conclusion that this man's suffering was the consequence of either his sin or that of his parents. Perhaps even more distressing than this flawed thinking is the inference that, because the disciples had not been born blind, they were more righteous than this man and his parents. Such a legalistic and hypocritical attitude will condemn us every time.

In my early years of ministry, I was an associate pastor under a leader who had served the same church for over twenty-five years. Generously, unselfishly, and lovingly his wife had shared her own life as well as her husband with the people of that city and church. Then she became terminally ill with cancer. The real tragedy was not her death, but the emotional pain caused by a church member who marched into the hospital room to inform this dying woman that it was her own fault that she had cancer. The accuser tried to play God.

Often our heavenly Father permits fiery trials to build the faith of His children, to purify them as gold, to prepare them for future service, or to give them the privilege of suffering for Christ's sake. If unusual suffering could always be traced back to gross sin, Jesus would have been the worst sinner in history.

And what about the Christian martyrs who were burned at the stake, torn apart by wild animals, stoned, and crucified? Would you accuse them of being singled out by God for their secret sin? Who are we to say that people who writhe in pain, who are plunged into deepest grief, or who wrestle with severe depression are being punished by God? Genuine punishment for sin, Jesus implied, belongs to the next world, not this one. So we must refuse to draw unfavorable conclusions about people in adverse circumstances.

SUFFERING SHOULD MAKE US REPENT

In Luke 13:1–5, Jesus went a step beyond exhorting us to get our eyes off of others. He also urged us to look at ourselves: "Unless you repent, you will all likewise perish" (vv. 3, 5). When disaster hits someone else, we should say to ourselves, "My sins deserve that severe treatment and much more. This is a picture of what could happen to me spiritually if I'm not right with God." Then we should pray, "Lord, show me the unconfessed sins in my life. I know they displease You. I want to turn away from them and back toward You."

This is what repentance is all about. The Greek *metanoeō,* commonly translated "repentance," literally means "to change one's mind."[3] To repent, we must change our minds about several things. First, we must radically alter our thinking about ourselves. We used to think we were basically good. But now that the Spirit has convicted us we see ourselves as sinners. In times past we imagined we were self-sufficient. Now we realize that we need a Savior.

Second, repentance changes our minds about sin. We used to make excuses for actions that hurt others and ourselves. We believed in situation ethics—that no action is absolutely right or wrong; rather, it all depends on the situation. For example, if a man and a woman have sexual relations outside of marriage, situation ethics would say that as long as they love each other, they are not guilty of adultery or fornication. Or if you tell a lie to avoid hurting someone's feelings, you are doing the right thing. Repentance sweeps all those bogus excuses away. It compels us to agree with God that sin is sin, merely because He says so in His Word.

To "agree" or "admit" to something is the basic meaning of the Greek verb *homologeō,* which is commonly translated "confess."[4] It literally means "to say the same thing."[5] In confession we say the same thing about sin that God says, namely, that it's wrong, that it involves guilt, and that it needs to be forsaken. Only people who have repented—that is, who have changed their minds about sin—can make confession to God in the biblical sense.

Third, repentance implies a change of mind about Christ. Perhaps in the past you used His name as a curse. Now it has become the melody of your hymns, the standard for your prayers, the theme of your testimony, and the strength of your life. Formerly Jesus was nothing to you, but now He is your Savior, your Lord, your All-in-all. You have experienced a profound change of attitude concerning Jesus. That's what repentance is all about.

Here, then, is a summary definition of repentance. *Repentance is a change of mind that leads to a change of heart that proves itself in a changed life.*[6] Counterfeit repentance dreads the consequences of sin. It is like the little girl who prayed, "O God, make me good. But not too good. Just good enough that I won't have to get spanked."

Or take the case of an unmarried teenage girl who becomes pregnant. Her peers at school ridicule her. A new boy whom she likes won't come near her, because she is "marked." She feels she cannot get on with her life until she has the baby and gives it up for adoption. Does she regret her sin of being sexually promiscuous? She may be sorry only that she has to bear the consequences of her moral indiscretion.

These are examples of false repentance. Genuine repentance involves a heart broken *for* and *from* sin, and it leads to a radical transformation in the way one thinks and acts.

Action Steps

We would be remiss if we merely studied Luke 13:1–5, understood its background, and learned from its insights. Twice in these verses our Lord challenges us with these words: "Unless you repent . . ." The pronoun *you* refers to more than Jesus' original first-century hearers. Today Jesus speaks these same words to *us*.

So let's ask, "Of what do I need to repent? What does the Holy Spirit desire to remove from my heart and life?" Possibly it's an unforgiving attitude toward someone who has offended you. Maybe secret lust has grown like a weed for years in the carnal soil of your heart. Perhaps neglect of God's Word, lack of prayer, shame that has prevented you from speaking to others about Christ, or temper outbursts have been destroying your relationships, despite your denials that they have been a serious problem.

You might wonder whether repentance is proper for Christians. Most certainly as long as we keep sinning we must continue to repent. Every day we need to say no to sin and yes to God.

In the deepest sense, Jesus' words urge us not to presume that we belong to God. Twice Christ warned, "Unless you repent, you will all likewise perish" (vv. 3, 5). In recent years Bible scholars have debated whether repentance is necessary for salvation. Those who claim it is not have failed to reckon with this text. I fear that many church members are what the Puritans called "gospel hypocrites"—people who assume their salvation is secure because they have registered an intellectual vote of confidence in Jesus as the Savior of the world. But they have never turned from sin and committed themselves to Christ. They are perishing.

Please don't tell me that you've been baptized. Don't tell me that you're a member of the church. Don't tell me that you teach a Bible study class. Instead, tell me that you've been spiritually transformed by Christ. Tell me that you hate the sin you used to love and that you love the Lord you used to despise. Tell me that you're a new person from the inside out. Tell me that you've repented. Then I'll tell you that you've responded positively to Jesus' intriguing question.

Study Guide

1. Read Luke 13:1–5. Was Jesus saying that the Galileans Pilate murdered and those killed by the tower were innocent? If not, what was He saying about their sinfulness?

2. How would you describe sin to someone who is unacquainted with the Bible?

3. In God's eyes, is the sin of adultery worse than the sin of worry? Are there degrees of sin, or is all sin the same? What do Matthew 11:23–24, Luke 12:47–48, and 1 John 5:16–17 imply about this?

4. When people suffer from cancer, HIV, the tragic death of a family member, or a divorce, is God punishing them for sin in their lives? What is the connection between suffering and sin?

5. Repentance literally means "to change one's mind." In what ways have you changed your mind about yourself, sin, and Jesus since becoming a Christian?

6. What do these verses teach about repentance?

   • Luke 24:47

   • Acts 11:18

   • Acts 17:30

   • Acts 26:20

   • Romans 2:4

   • 2 Timothy 2:25

   • 2 Peter 3:9

7. Twice in Luke 13:1–5, Jesus used the Greek word rendered "perish" (vv. 3, 5). Also note the word translated "perish" or "perishing" in John 3:16; 10:28; 1 Corinthians 1:18; 2 Corinthians 2:15; 2 Thessalonians 2:10; and 2 Peter 3:9. What does it means for a person to perish?

8. Read 2 Corinthians 7:9–10, which draws a distinction between worldly sorrow and godly repentance. What is that difference? How does repentance go beyond feeling sorry or remorseful for your sinful actions?

9. On the night of Jesus' arrest, Peter denied Him three times (Matt. 26:69–75), and Judas betrayed Him (vv. 47–56). Both men were troubled by their actions (26:75; 27:3–5), but only Peter turned to Christ in faith for forgiveness. Why? What was the difference between Peter's and Judas's responses to their respective sins against Jesus?

A BREATHTAKING QUESTION:

"What is the kingdom of God like?" (Luke 13:18)

YOU SELDOM SEE RESIDENTS OF a retirement home springing backflips down the hallway. Retired pastor Wilbur Westerdahl didn't go that far, but he put on quite a show for his fellow residents of Covenant Village. He had just read a newspaper interview about me, in which I was asked the question, "How did you become interested in pastoral ministry?"

I spoke about my love for Pastor Westerdahl when I was five years old. I explained, "Every Sunday while leaving church, I would remind him, 'I'm going to be just like you when I grow up!'

"He got sick of hearing that, so he told me, 'From now on, just wink at me each Sunday, and I'll know that means you still want to be a pastor when you grow up.' For years I winked and grinned as I shook my pastor's hand after church each week. God used my love for that man to call me into the ministry."

I suppose that years ago Pastor Westerdahl took with a grain of salt the promises of that five-year-old pest. But in the end it was as if I was to carry on his life's work. He was richly blessed by the reminder that surprising results flow from insignificant beginnings.

In 1849, seventeen-year-old James Hudson Taylor felt a keen sense of God's calling to the mission field of China. Five years later he landed at Shanghai. Other missionaries considered him "a poor, unconnected nobody." Because no mission was willing to back him, Taylor founded the China Inland Mission. He prayed that God would send him "twenty-four willing, skillful laborers," two for each unreached province. His goal was nothing less than to bring the gospel to every person in China.

At first the China Inland Mission was opposed by fellow missionaries as well as by the Chinese. Some riots even broke out against Taylor and his associates. Less than thirty years after his mission began, Taylor led 641 missionaries, about half the entire Protestant force in China. Today the China Inland Mission continues under the name of Overseas Missionary Fellowship. Many other mission stations have been founded as a result of it, and countless Christians have been called to foreign fields as a result of the influence of Taylor.

Small and insignificant beginnings can lead to undreamed-of results. Jesus illustrated this truth in His parables of the mustard seed and the leaven. He introduced them by similar breathtaking questions: "What is the kingdom of God like?" (Luke 13:18), and, "To what shall I compare the kingdom of God?" (v. 20). Jesus taught more about the divine kingdom than anything else. Through the forty days between His resurrection and ascension, His teaching seems to have been focused on this subject (Acts 1:3).

In these parables of the mustard seed and the leaven, our Lord encouraged despairing hearts with two facts about God's kingdom.

EVEN SMALL KINGDOM WORK IS SIGNIFICANT

Jesus compared God's kingdom to "a mustard seed, which a man took and threw into his own garden; and it grew and became a tree; and the birds of the air nested in its branches" (Luke 13:19). The mustard seed was the smallest of all seeds used in Palestine. It was difficult to see one by itself, for it was about the size of the head of a pin. A person could hold thousands in the palm of his or her hand. Yet just one of them could mature into a tree in which birds made their nests. This reminds me of a maxim: "Great oaks grow from little acorns."

Our Lord takes us by surprise when He compares the kingdom of God to a mustard seed. We would expect Him to compare it to something vast, such as the Mediterranean Sea or the Roman Empire. But instead He chooses something almost microscopic.

In Sabine Baring-Gould's 1864 hymn, "Onward Christian Soldiers," we sing, "Like a mighty army moves the church of God." But Jesus says the kingdom, of which the church is a part, grows more like a tiny seed. It may become large, but it always begins small. God sets no value on ostentation. He loves to work through what appear to be paltry people and trifling events. And the result is a changed world.

This was encouraging news to the disciples. They had left their families to follow Jesus and given up their careers to become evangelists. But what did they have to show for it? They reaped the animosity of the Jewish religious leaders, the disgust of the Roman Empire, and the threat of martyrdom. Sure, many sick people were being healed, and crowds of people were blessed. But some of the disciples' dreams of overthrowing the political yoke of Rome and being lauded as heroes were quickly turning to nightmares. Perhaps a few of them were beginning to wonder, "Is our allegiance to Jesus worth all this?"

I can imagine Jesus telling them, "Remember the mustard seed! Though it appears insignificantly small, it is filled with life. When planted, it will inevitably grow into a tree that birds call their home. So don't be discouraged!"

Possibly you are serving Christ in a tiny patch of His vineyard. Maybe your church is unable to afford a full-time pastor, or perhaps your Bible study group is made up of just a handful of people. You might wonder whether your labors for Christ make any difference in His kingdom. Don't forget the mustard seed! Kingdom work always begins small, and its significance derives not from its size but from its intrinsic life.

Unlike the first disciples, we can see the proof of what Jesus said in Luke 13:19. He Himself was born in obscurity. His hometown of Nazareth was so insignificant that one Jew (Nathanael) questioned whether anything good could come from it (John 1:46). Jesus lived in poverty, possessed no formal religious training, and never wrote a book. He was rejected by other Jews. In fact, they and the Romans crucified Him. But Christ's burial was like the planting of a mustard seed. Soon He was alive again, and in the centuries following His resurrection, ascension, and exaltation, people have flocked to Him in faith like birds to the branches of a tree.

Again, consider the apostles. How could a mere twelve men "make disciples of all the nations" (Matt. 28:19)? Jesus Himself called them a "little flock" (Luke 12:32). The religious leaders of that day pegged them as "uneducated and untrained men" (Acts 4:13). After the ascension of their Lord, the number of those who remained together totaled about 120 people (1:15). On Pentecost, three thousand converts were added (2:41). The number soon grew to over five thousand (4:4). And from then on "the number of the disciples continued to increase greatly" (6:7).

Despite outward persecution and inward hardness of heart from the unsaved people the early Christians were trying to reach, God's kingdom swelled with new citizens. Shortly after the start of the third century, the African theologian Tertullian could write to the Roman Emperor, "We Christians have filled everything that is yours—your cities, islands, free towns, castles, council halls, the palace, the senate, and the forum, all classes of men. We outnumber your armies. There are more Christians in a single province than men in all your legions."

In Revelation 7:9 we read that at the end of the age believers in Christ will be "a great multitude, which no one could count, from every nation and all tribes and peoples and tongues." This reminds us that nothing can stop the progress of the gospel. Like a mustard seed, it is infused with life that by its very nature *must* grow.

So don't lose heart when the ministry you're involved in seems too small to make a difference. Jesus had a knack for finding value in little things—for example, the widow's mite, the one talent, the cup of cold water, and a boy's lunch for the feeding of five thousand.

Years ago in our church's midweek children's ministry, one of our teachers introduced a young boy named Todd Burkdoll to Christ. Little did that teacher dream that fifteen years later Todd would take the gospel as a missionary to Thailand. The mustard seed of faith grew into a large tree!

By 1515, a Catholic monk and university professor named Martin Luther had been changed by the words of Romans 1:17: "The just shall live by faith" (KJV). He came to see that salvation was a free gift meant to be received by faith. By 1517 Luther was protesting against the Roman Catholic teaching that salvation is to be earned by good works. Like a tiny grain of mustard seed, Martin Luther, filled with the life of God's Word, single-handedly sparked the Protestant Reformation. Many Christians continue to make their spiritual nests in its branches.

I believe that we are making history right now. In heaven we will look back and see how even some of our casual remarks spoken in Christ's name served as a catalyst that transformed the lives of others and compelled them to change the world through the gospel.

Many think that Jesus' mention of the birds of the sky nesting in the branches of the mustard tree was a prophecy of the Gentiles entering God's kingdom. Some unbelievers sarcastically remark, "Christianity is for the birds!" Little do they realize that Jesus agrees with them! The song of heaven is that Christ has purchased with His blood individuals "from every tribe and tongue and people and nation" (Rev. 5:9).

Therefore, any trace of segregation in our churches is out of place. In Christ there are no racial, social, spiritual, or personal distinctions (Gal. 3:28). None of us has the right to insist that others in the body of Christ dress like us, practice our style of worship, read from our favorite version of Scripture, belong to our denomination, or agree on insignificant points of doctrine. It is not just the robins that nest in the branches of the mustard tree, but also the blue jays, the sparrows, the cardinals, and any other birds that wish. The kingdom of God is large enough for us all. It is destined to take in multitudes of people from every walk of life, for its living seed causes it to grow.

Unnoticed Kingdom Work Transforms Society

Luke 13:20–21 contains another parable about the kingdom: "And again [Jesus] said, 'To what shall I compare the kingdom of God? It is like leaven, which a woman took and hid in three pecks of meal, until it was all leavened.'" Leaven is a substance used to produce fermentation in dough.

Some Bible teachers insist that throughout Scripture leaven is always a symbol of evil.[1] And yet when the Jews offered their peace offerings for thanksgiving, the Lord ordered them to present leavened bread (Lev. 7:13). Their wave offerings were also to be "baked with leaven" (23:17). This indicates that leaven doesn't always represent something evil.

The same symbols can be used in differing Scripture contexts to represent quite different things. For example, the Bible describes both Satan (1 Peter 5:8) and Jesus (Rev. 5:5) as a lion. A serpent represents Satan (Gen. 3:1; Rev. 12:9), and also believers (Matt. 10:16). So it is with leaven, which does not have a uniform symbolic meaning in the Bible. We must interpret each occurrence by its own distinctions. In Luke 13:20–21, Jesus said the kingdom of God (*not* the kingdom of Satan) is like leaven. The context dictates that we must interpret the leaven as symbolizing that which is good. If it represented the demonic influences that would invade the church in later years, our Lord would have used the future tense ("the kingdom of God *will* be like"). Instead, He used the present tense ("*is* like"). Moreover, if leaven were a corrupting influence in this parable, Jesus would be implying that in the end God's kingdom will fail.

This parable is a counterpart to the previous one. The mustard seed illustrates the outward growth of God's kingdom; the leaven portrays its ability to transform society from the inside out.

When the baby Jesus was born in Bethlehem, it was as if God blended a tiny piece of leaven into the mass of humankind. And look what became of it. Jesus' life worked a metamorphosis in the lives of the twelve disciples. They, in turn, "turned the world upside down" (Acts 17:6 KJV). Nearly two thousand years later the leaven of the gospel continues to transform society. And one day this shout will be heard in heaven: "The kingdom of the world has become the kingdom of our Lord, and of His Christ" (Rev. 11:15).

On a more individual level we could say that God kneads the leaven of His Holy Spirit into the dough of the hearts of new converts, and He begins to alter every part of them. That "leaven" influences their marriages, their families, and even their business ethics. Just as leaven turns dough into a seething mass, so the Holy Spirit, planted in the hearts of Christians, overthrows their sinful habits. When these leavened people are out of fellowship with God, they find they cannot rest until they confess and repent of their sin.

Israel's King David serves as an example. While he tried to conceal his sins of adultery and murder, his body wasted away and he lost his vitality (Ps. 32:3–4). David was miserable because the leaven of new life within him would not allow him to relax in his sin. Like a batch of dough under the influence of leaven, David's spirit was aching.

Is the Spirit gaining control over you? Or is there a corner of your life where His access is forbidden? Leaven persists until it transforms the whole lump of dough. And God's Spirit will persevere until He has all of you. At times His work will strain you, like leaven that causes dough to rise and expand. But in the end you'll resemble Christ, the very bread of heaven.

The leavening influence initially begins with God's work on your character. Once the Lord has leavened you, He calls you to be His leaven in the world. His will is that for Christ's sake you positively influence everything around you. God wants you to be transformed and a transformer of others by His grace.

One evening some members of our congregation and I appeared before the city council to request permission to construct a new church building on vacant land we owned. After much discussion, we received the official go-ahead. More than a year later a woman worshiped with us for the first time. Later that week I visited in her home and learned that she had not attended church in years. When I asked her what moved her to come, she answered, "Last year you and some of your members appeared before the city council to request a building permit for your new church! I was there that night, too, and something about you people rubbed off on me. All these months I couldn't forget it. It made me want to be part of you, so here I am."

What was it about us that rubbed off on that woman? The leaven of our witness. Its nature is to change people who come into contact with it. That evening at city hall we had no idea that God was using us, but He did!

Perhaps you are unsure whether the Lord is using you. If so, encourage yourself in the knowledge that the leaven of God works invisibly and mysteriously to change the dough of the hearts you touch with the gospel. Sometimes only God can see the positive results of our witness for Christ. But when He sees it, we don't have to.

You may ask, "What about the people to whom I witness who never change? Why does the leaven of the gospel fail to work on them?" Sometimes the people to whom you witness are not like soft dough. Their hearts have already become crusty and hard, making it impossible for the spiritual leaven to be kneaded into them. But Jesus' parable of the four soils promises that some hearts are ready for the gospel seed. In those cases, all you need to do is yield yourself to the Spirit and so be His transforming agent.

Action Steps

The parables of the mustard seed and the leaven drive home to us three key lessons, and each one suggests an action step we can take. The first lesson is that the life and power of God's kingdom have already been unleashed. Maybe your service for Christ is more like a mustard seed than a tree and more like a pinch of leaven than a transformed batch of dough. But don't despair; even a mustard seed has life in it, and that pinch of leaven is packed with power. So expect God to use you now.

The title of George Ladd's book on the kingdom of God, *The Presence of the Future,* reminds us that we don't have to wait until the millennial reign of Christ to see the kingdom in operation.[2] All its life and power are germinating even now. So ask your Lord to manifest that life and power through you.

Second, Jesus' two parables admonish us to be patient with the work of God. Until Christ returns, the mustard seed will continue to grow and the leaven's influence will be incomplete. So don't be frustrated if that family member or friend makes little or no progress toward conversion. Didn't God wait for many years for you to become a Christian? Be patient with others who hesitate to trust in Christ for salvation. Don't underestimate the tiny steps they take toward placing their faith in Christ. Instead, see those steps as evidences of God's kingdom at work, for mustard seeds and leaven by nature are small.

Third, the mustard seed and the leaven illustrate that God wants to transform the world spiritually. As a member of the kingdom, are you an agent of God's change, or is the world changing you? Scripture cautions us, "Don't let the world around you squeeze you into its own mold, but let God remold your minds from within" (Rom. 12:2 PH).

Jesus warned us that as the salt of the earth, we can become tasteless (Matt. 5:13). In a similar way, we must face the possibility that we have lost our leavening influence. Earlier I said our witness for Christ is sometimes ineffective because the hearts of many are hard and thus unable to be kneaded with the leaven of the gospel. But another reason we see so few people change is that we do not live as spiritually leavening agents. We abandoned that role when we said yes to worldliness.

Is the mustard seed of God's kingdom in your heart? Then plant it as a new work for Christ in your sphere of influence. Has the good news of Christ's substitutionary death on the cross spiritually leavened your life? Then be God's leaven in the life of someone else. However small your kingdom work, its seed of life and its germ of power can accomplish enormous results—all for the salvation of people, the growth of Christ's church, and the glory of God!

Study Guide

1. The parables of the mustard seed and the leaven teach us that kingdom work in this world begins small. Share an experience when you were involved in a service for Christ that was so small, you wondered whether it had significance. Now that you can look back on that service, what significance, if any, can you see in it?

2. The parables of the mustard seed and the leaven teach us that surprising results can flow from insignificant beginnings. At the opening of this chapter, I gave two examples of this principle. Share another example from your own life, the life of someone you know, current events, or history.

3. What tiny mustard seed planted in your heart (a verse of Scripture, a remark in a sermon, a Christian song or hymn, or someone's example) eventually changed your life?

4. The parables of the mustard seed and the leaven illustrate that God wants to spiritually transform the world. In what specific way does Jesus want you to be His agent of change in someone's life or in society?

5. The opposite of being Jesus' agent of change in this world is to allow the world to change you. In what subtle ways does the spirit of worldliness seek to dull your cutting edge for Christ?

6. In each passage below, what warning does God give us about the world?

   • Romans 12:2

   • James 1:27

   • James 4:4

   • 1 John 2:15–17

7. A mustard seed is planted underground and leaven works invisibly from within to transform the dough. Give an example of a specific ministry for Christ that takes place behind the scenes and out of the spotlight. This ministry might be in your church, in a parachurch ministry, or in the surrounding community.

8. The work of the mustard seed and leaven will be incomplete until Jesus returns. That means we must serve Christ patiently. In what area of your life is God teaching you to be patient?

9. What do these verses teach about patience?

    • Ecclesiastes 7:8

    • 1 Corinthians 13:4

    • Galatians 5:22

    • Colossians 3:12–13

    • 1 Thessalonians 5:14

    • 2 Timothy 2:24

    • Hebrews 6:11–12

10. The parables of the mustard seed and the leaven illustrate the king-
    dom of God—the subject about which Jesus taught more than any
    other during His earthly ministry. What do you think is implied
    in having Jesus as the King of your life?

11. As one of the "birds" nesting in the branches of God's kingdom,
    what would you say is so inviting about it?

A PRACTICAL QUESTION:

"Which one of you, when he wants to build a tower, does not first sit down and calculate the cost to see if he has enough to complete it?" (Luke 14:28)

IT WAS THE MOST RIDICULOUS thing I've ever seen. As I drove north on highway 101 in California to visit my parents, there it was, spanning the freeway in the middle of San Jose—a giant overpass that led nowhere in two directions. It was begun as an artery that was supposed to connect highway 101 to another freeway. But for years it stood there half-finished. Every time I drove under the freeway that had two shoulders and no arms, I had to shake my head and laugh. I learned a valuable lesson from that eyesore: A job half done exposes people to more ridicule than a job never begun.

How many unfinished jobs do you have around your house? Perhaps you purchased a new swing set for the kids. But when you tried to read the instructions, you felt only a rocket scientist could understand them. The swing set is still boxed up in the garage rather than assembled in the backyard. Your children ask, "When are you going to put up our swing set?" And every excuse reminds you that you are a dreamer but not a finisher.

Possibly you started to write a letter to a friend who is suffering through a divorce. After two or three sentences you didn't know what else to say, so you put down your pen. You intend to finish when a wave of inspiration passes over you, but the waters have been calm. That half-written letter was meant to encourage your friend, but now it discourages you.

Or perhaps last New Year's Eve you resolved to read your Bible from cover to cover during the calendar year. At the pace of fifteen minutes a day you could accomplish your goal. You were on schedule through the middle of February, but then you stopped. Your bookmark is still in Leviticus, and your spirit is bone-dry.

In Luke 14:28–32, Jesus asked two practical questions that challenge us to go the distance in our walk with Him.

COUNT THE COST OF FOLLOWING CHRIST

At this stage in Jesus' ministry, His popularity was soaring. We read that "great multitudes were going along with Him" (v. 25). We could paraphrase, "They were going along for the ride." These were curiosity seekers and spectators, people who would jump in the car and follow the fire truck when they hear its siren.

Jesus asked them, "Which one of you, when he wants to build a tower, does not first sit down and calculate the cost, to see if he has enough to complete it?" (v. 28). Towers were usually built in vineyards as lookout posts from which to spot thieves who would steal the harvest and animals that would damage the crops.[1] Towers were worthy projects. As a carpenter, Jesus had probably built some.

In verse 33, Jesus implied that there is a parallel between the tower and the product of a disciple's spiritual life. A tower stands tall and is an unusual type of building. Likewise, a disciple should stand out as different. Everyone is building a life of some kind. What does your structure look like? A shack? A house that fits into the neighborhood of the world? Or a tower that points to heaven?

Towers, of course, are expensive. So Jesus commanded us to count the cost of discipleship.

"Isn't salvation free?" you may ask. "What's all this talk about a price I have to pay?"

Yes, salvation is free. Scripture clearly teaches that "the free gift of God is eternal life in Christ Jesus our Lord" (Rom. 6:23). How, then, can Jesus warn us to count the cost of discipleship? This has been one of the most hotly debated issues in Christian circles in recent years.

Suppose a father takes his son into their garage on his birthday. As he walks in, the son sees a shiny new car, and his father shouts, "Happy birthday!" The car is his gift to his son, who pays nothing to receive it. But operating that car will be another story. The young man must now get a job, because he will have to dish out his own money when his car needs gas, maintenance, repairs, insurance, and registration fees. Owning a car is expensive.

Some drivers try to get by on bare minimums. They skip the costs of maintenance and repairs, not to mention insurance and sometimes even registration fees. Consequently, their cars cough and sputter, stall and break down. Many Christians try to get by without paying the cost of discipleship. They are spectators in church but not soldiers on the battlefield. They come along for the ride but don't pull their own weight. They may be believers, but they are not disciples.

William Barclay tells a story about a man who said to a professor, "I hear that so-and-so was one of your students." The professor replied, "No. He attended my lectures, but he was not one of my students."[2]

The meaning of the word *disciple* is "learner."[3] What would Jesus say about you? "She listened to sermons for decades, but she never learned anything; she is no disciple of Mine."

Whenever I conduct a marriage ceremony, I remind the wedding guests that "marriage is not to be entered into lightly, but rather reverently, advisedly, with a sound mind, and in the fear of God." Engaged couples should count the cost of getting married, yet many don't. They are just as married as the couples who prepare conscientiously for marriage and commit themselves to living in love. But the couples who rush into marriage have much more difficulty making it work.

Every Christian is married to Jesus, but not every Christian has counted the cost of living for Christ day in and day out. The word "cost" in Luke 14:28 shows that Jesus was talking about estimating the expense of discipleship.[4]

The church I serve as pastor recently constructed a new facility from the ground up at a new location. We discovered that there were endless costs—the land, the plans, the fees, the permits, the improvements to the land, the contractors, and the structure. For eight years we planned, worked, gathered information, talked to contractors, met with public officials, applied for permits—and we still hadn't even broken ground! There is a high cost—financially and otherwise—to any building program.

And what is the cost of discipleship? First, *it will cost us our loyalties.* Jesus said, "If anyone comes to Me, and does not hate his own father and mother and wife and children and brothers and sisters, yes, and even his own life, he cannot be My disciple" (v. 26). Commentators agree that in this verse our Lord was using hyperbole, or intentional exaggeration. The parallel verse in Matthew 10:37 confirms this. There Jesus told us not to love father, mother, son, or daughter more than Him. Our loyalty to Christ must surpass the loyalty we show to those who are nearest and dearest to us. If we are ever forced to choose between our allegiance to Christ and our allegiance to family members, we must not hesitate to side with our Lord.

I have known husbands and wives who lost spouses because of this change in loyalties. Before their conversion, these men and women indulged in sin with their mates. But after giving their lives to Christ they took a stand against unrighteousness. In one case the issue was drunkenness; in another it was wife swapping; in another it was abortion. When they refused to take part in these sins, they were traded for other partners. They counted the cost of discipleship and were willing to pay it.

Second, *discipleship to Jesus will cost us our lives.* Our Lord warned us, "Whoever does not carry his own cross and come after Me cannot be My disciple" (Luke 14:27). What does bearing the cross involve? Much more than bearing a burden. Sometimes believers will say, "My unwanted divorce is the cross I carry" or "My cross is a rebellious son." But Jesus' demand that we take up the cross implies that it is something we can avoid but should not. Divorce and a rebellious child are things that Christ wants us to do our part to try to avoid.

The cross we must take up, therefore, is the suffering we could escape if we were willing to compromise our faith. Disciples choose to suffer rather than compromise. In Jesus' day crosses were used exclusively for one purpose—to execute people.[5] Our Lord was telling us, "If you want to be My disciple, you must be willing to die for Me." The first words of Dietrich Bonhoeffer in his classic book *The Cost of Discipleship* are, "When Christ calls a man, he bids him come and die."

Our willingness to die physically for Christ must be practiced spiritually every day. Paul testified, "I die daily" (1 Cor. 15:31). Each new morning Paul mounted the cross, so to speak, and put self to death so that Christ might live through him. Paul had counted the cost of discipleship and was willing to pay it.

Jesus died on the cross to cleanse us from sin. That implies that *taking up our crosses means we are willing to part with sin.* This is the third cost of discipleship. Isaiah 55:7 says, "Let the wicked forsake his way." In the New Testament we are told to "live the rest of the time in the flesh no longer for the lusts of men, but for the will of God" (1 Peter 4:2).

Disciples are liberated people. In Christ they practice freedom from extramarital sex, profanity, jealousy, outbursts of temper, drunkenness, greed, and gossip. They aren't perfect, but neither are they under bondage to sin. The problem with many people is not that they are slaves to sin, but that they don't want to be freed from it. They are content to live in bondage to sin, and they don't want to be disturbed. Such people injure the cause of Christ when they call themselves His followers, for they have never counted the cost of discipleship. They are responsible for the accusations of hypocrisy that the world heaps on the church.

Jesus compares such hypocrites to the man who failed to calculate the cost of building his tower: "When he has laid a foundation, and is not able to finish, all who observe it begin to ridicule him, saying, 'This man began to build and was not able to finish'" (Luke 14:29–30). By definition, a tower stands tall above everything else. So when the builder completed only its foundation, he made himself a target for ridicule.

If you want Satan to mock you, follow Christ without counting the cost. Your family and friends will be skeptical when you declare your allegiance to Christ. There will be no end to the fun they poke at you if you flunk out of the discipleship course. They will laugh and say, "We told you this was only a phase you were passing through. We knew you'd come back to your old life. You wouldn't admit your Christian commitment was only a fad; you insisted it would last. But now we know the truth, don't we?"

In the Old Testament, following the Lord cost Abraham his home. It cost Joseph two years in prison for a crime he didn't commit. It cost Moses all the riches of Egypt. It cost Shadrach, Meshach, and Abednego some time in a furnace of fire. It cost Daniel a night in a lions' den. In the New Testament, following Christ cost Stephen his life by stoning. It cost Paul his family, his friends, and his reputation. It cost John an exile to the Island of Patmos.

Possibly when you were converted, you didn't count the cost of following Christ. All you knew was that you were receiving forgiveness for your sins, an eternal home in heaven, and Jesus in your life. Maybe you have completely overlooked the cost of discipleship. But what will you do about it now? Is Jesus just a convenience to you? Is your relationship to Him one-sided, with the commitment coming only from Him? Or have you surrendered to Him total authority over your decisions, plans, finances, goals, and career?

When Julius Caesar landed on the shores of Britain with his Roman legions, he ordered his men to halt on the edge of the cliffs of Dover and look down to the water below. They were shocked to see every ship set ablaze in which they had crossed the English Channel. Caesar had made it impossible for them to retreat. There was nothing left to do but advance and conquer. His warriors may not have counted the cost of service when they signed up, but they were going to pay it now.

Christ wants you to burn your bridges of sin behind you. Each time a temptation stares you in the face, you are not to ask yourself, "Should I, or shouldn't I?" You are to say, "I must not yield to this, because I have already given my life to Christ." If you are a college student and professors mock your belief in Scripture, you are not to weigh their arguments and make a fresh decision for or against Christ. God wants you to tell that professor, "It's too late to try to destroy my faith. I've already set it in concrete." That is the mind-set of a disciple.

COUNT THE COST OF NOT FOLLOWING CHRIST

Now, by means of a second question, our Lord asks us to count the cost of not following Him: "Or what king, when he sets out to meet another king in battle, will not first sit down and take counsel whether he is strong enough with ten thousand men to encounter the one coming against him with twenty thousand? Or else, while the other is still far away, he sends a delegation and asks terms of peace" (Luke 14:31–32).

The man who considered building the tower was under no constraint to do so. It was a good idea, but he had other alternatives. He could have stationed guards all around his vineyard and achieved the same result. But the king who went to war had no choice. Jesus says his enemy was already "coming against him with twenty thousand" warriors. The king's only options were to fight or surrender. He couldn't remain neutral.

We, too, have an enemy. His name is Satan. He is coming against us with all the hosts of hell, and we can't hold him back. As Paul reminds us in Ephesians 6:12, "Our struggle is not against flesh and blood, but against the rulers, against the powers, against the world forces of this darkness, against the spiritual forces of wickedness in the heavenly places." Like the king in Jesus' parable, we have two choices. We can wage war against the Devil, or we can surrender to him.

In our own strength we're no match for Satan, any more than a king with ten soldiers stands a chance of conquering an enemy with ten million. But one person plus Jesus Christ is always a majority. If we commit ourselves to Him, He will be our defense. More than that, "we overwhelmingly conquer through Him who loved us" (Rom. 8:37).

Consequently, the cost of not surrendering to the Lord is to capitulate to Satan. And the cost of not following Christ is to submit to the Devil. You cannot remain neutral. If you don't enlist with Jesus Christ, you will default to Satan. Are you willing to pay that price?

Dwight Small wrote a popular book entitled *The High Cost of Holy Living*. Perhaps the sequel could have been entitled *The High Cost of Unholy Living*. It costs plenty not to be a committed Christian—so much so that we are unable to pay off the debt of sin by ourselves. As a result, Satan takes it out on our families and friends. The sins we commit in bondage to him hurt the people we love, who pay for our lack of discipleship with broken hearts and scarred lives. The cost of not following Christ is devastation to people all around us.

If we think we can choose between serving Christ and serving ourselves, we are deceived. The real choice is between serving the Lord and serving the Devil. The best we can do is to become slaves of the right master. And in so doing, we find our greatest freedom.

Action Steps

I'm fascinated by the fact that Jesus didn't tell us whether the tower was ever built or whether the king went to war rather than surrender to his enemy. All Jesus said was that the builder and the king thought through their options. Perhaps our Lord left their final actions unstated because He wants *us* to write the ending to His stories.

We are the builder, and we face the battle. What will we do now—pay the cost of discipleship or sell out to Satan? That is the challenge of this passage. The great Bible teacher, G. Campbell Morgan, said he never read Luke 14:28–32 without wondering if he was a disciple at all.[6] You and I owe it to ourselves to consider soberly that same question. And then we owe it to the One we call Lord to give Him total commitment.

Jesus' challenge seems to repel some readers. It's as if He were saying, "Go away from Me if you're not willing to count the cost of discipleship and pay it." That's a risky thing to say, except for one truth: The cost of discipleship becomes a privilege when we recall the cost of salvation that Jesus paid in full for us.

Our Lord directs us to give up our earthly loyalties, our cherished sins, and the control of our lives. But Christ went far beyond that. He gave up His home in heaven. He set aside His kingly privileges, took the form of a bond-servant, and became a human being. He obeyed the Father all the way to dying on a cross (Phil. 2:5–8). Jesus cheerfully paid for us the ultimate cost by shedding His own blood. Out of love for us He endured the wrath of God so that we could be forgiven (2 Cor. 5:21).

Jesus did not leave half done the job His Father had sent Him to complete. He was able to report to Him in prayer, "I have finished the work which You have given Me to do" (John 17:4 NKJV). No one will ever ridicule Jesus for an unfinished task. Satan cannot mock our Lord for coming to earth and failing to die at Calvary. Jesus was able to shout from the cross, "It is finished!" (John 19:30). He counted the cost of our salvation and paid it in full. There is no mortgage on our souls for us to pay off.

The only thing left for us to do is follow Christ down the road of commitment, service, and love. Though steep, that is the only road to abundant life and fullness of joy.

Study Guide

1. Jesus' two parables in Luke 14:28–32 emphasize the cost of discipleship. How do you explain the difference, if there is one, between the freedom of salvation and the cost of discipleship?

2. How would you answer an inquirer who asks, "What will it cost me to become Jesus' disciple?"

3. What did it cost you to become Jesus' disciple?

4. Immediately after His two parables, Jesus concluded, "So therefore, no one of you can be My disciple who does not give up all his own possessions" (v. 33). Are those words meant to be taken literally? If not, how do you interpret them?

5. What do these verses teach about the cost that Jesus paid to make you His disciple?

   * Isaiah 53:6

   * Matthew 27:46

   * Mark 10:45

   * 2 Corinthians 5:21

   * Philippians 2:6–8

6. Give an example of the sort of Christian who, like the builder in Luke 14:28–30, leaves work half done.

7. The word *disciple* means "learner." In these verses, what is involved in Christian learning?

   * Matthew 11:29

   * Matthew 28:20

   * Ephesians 4:20

   * Philippians 4:9

   * 2 Timothy 3:14

   * Titus 3:14

8. Share your personal experience about being trained as a disciple by someone else. How did it happen? How much time did it take? Or did no one nurture you personally in the Christian faith after your conversion?

9. The future of Christianity depends on current disciples making new disciples. Name someone in whose life you can spiritually reproduce yourself.

A MYSTERIOUS QUESTION:

"Did I Myself not choose you, the twelve, and yet one of you is a devil?" (John 6:70)

IT WOULD BE DIFFICULT TO THINK of a more notorious biblical villain than Judas Iscariot. Perhaps the only one who qualifies is the Devil. I don't know anyone by the name of Judas. It is too despicable. Even Jesus called him "a devil" (John 6:70). Judas performed the Devil's work by betraying Christ. That doesn't mean Judas was something other than human, for our Lord also called Peter "Satan" (Matt. 16:23).

Many readers of Scripture are perplexed by Jesus' question in John 6:70: "Did I Myself not choose you, the twelve, and yet one of you is a devil?" Why would Jesus invite a man into His company of disciples who would become a traitor? Let me suggest two reasons.

First, I believe our Lord regarded Judas as a potential follower. Jesus called him to discipleship just as sincerely as He called Peter, James, John, or the others. If Judas had responded to the love and teachings of Jesus, he could have been a pillar in the early church.

Second—and this is the other side of the mystery—Jesus enlisted Judas because He had to experience the summit of suffering in order to fulfill His role as Savior of the world. Not one stroke of God's wrath could be held back. Our Lord was required to experience it fully. What better way for Him to begin than by the traitorous kiss of a friend?

Husbands and wives who have caught their mates in the act of adultery know something of the agony Jesus must have felt when one of His own disciples interrupted His prayer time so that the chief priests could arrest Him. This was the first installment of unmitigated suffering that was fully unleashed on our Lord when He died on the cross as the sacrifice for our sins.

The question as to why Jesus chose Judas as His disciple is no more difficult to answer than this question: Why did He choose us? When Christ first looked upon us, did He see pure people? No. Like Judas, we possessed a devilish nature that wanted to seize for itself the glory that rightly belonged to God. Jesus chose Judas—and us—to be His followers, not because we had anything to offer Him, but because He had everything to offer us. We must trace back His choice ultimately to His own grace. Now let's consider six prominent lessons from the example of Judas.

SATAN WANTS TO INFILTRATE THE FELLOWSHIP OF BELIEVERS

If ever a group of believers was brought together to enjoy fellowship with Christ and one another, it was the Twelve. Mark 3:14 tells us that Jesus "appointed twelve, that they might be with Him." The primary purpose of this group was to bring its members into an intimate knowledge of Christ. According to John 17:3, this is what eternal life is all about.

We might have expected Satan to fear this group of which Jesus was the head. We might have thought this was the last fellowship in the world that the Devil wanted to join. To the contrary, it was the first. Jesus was going to commission these men to make disciples of all the nations (see Matt. 28:19). So if Satan was going to overthrow the work of Christ, his best chance was to nip his opposition in the bud by infiltrating the Twelve. Through Judas, the Devil got his foot in the door.

Guess where Satan's favorite place to hang out is now? Not the local bar; not the pornography shops; not the dens of prostitution. Satan goes to the church. You may occasionally miss a worship service, but the Devil doesn't. He is always present, sowing his seeds of discord among the believers. Whenever Christians meet for prayer, you'll also find the Devil there.

Have you been offended by another member of your church? Are you unreconciled with him or her as a result? The rift between you is no mere conflict of personalities; it is the work of Satan. Don't let another day pass before you seek out your brother or sister and make peace. The progress of the gospel depends on it.

Do you secretly despise people who attend a church that is different from yours? You'd never admit it, but perhaps you feel you can have no fellowship with believers who speak in tongues (or don't speak in tongues). You may wonder whether they are even believers at all, because they don't adopt your style of Christianity. Beware of such an attitude! It's nothing less than the fruit of satanic strategy.

A little girl asked her neighbor friend whether she could attend church with her on Sunday. The second girl said she would have to ask her mother. After doing so, she replied to her friend, "Mommy said I can't go to church with you, because we belong to a different abominations."

Exactly! Satan knows he can make a laughingstock out of us if he can only divide us. If we must have denominations, let's graciously accept the others that exalt the Christ of the Bible. To draw up ranks against each other is to accomplish the Devil's purpose for him.

HYPOCRITES ARE HARD TO SPOT

When Jesus informed His disciples that one of them was a devil, the other eleven didn't look askance at Judas, as if to say, "We know good and well who that devil is!" If they had known, we can be sure they would have ganged up on Judas right there. But the entire group was dumbfounded. They had often failed to understand Jesus' parables, and perhaps they assumed this was another of His obscure sayings. At this early stage even Judas himself likely did not know that Jesus was referring to him.

Among the Twelve there was only one office—that of treasurer—and it was held by Judas. The main quality people want in someone who handles their money is honesty. The disciples thought they had found it in Judas. They trusted him to the end.

The night of Jesus' arrest, He predicted, "Truly, truly, I say to you, that one of you will betray Me" (John 13:21). Verse 22 reports that "the disciples began looking at one another, at a loss to know of which one He was speaking." Imagine, after three years of living with Judas, they still didn't know he was the traitor. Judas acted like Satan; he also acted like an apostle of Jesus. Don't expect to recognize the hypocrisy in every phony who comes along. Even in heaven we'll be surprised at the absence of people we now assume will be there.

YOU MUST GUARD AGAINST HYPOCRISY

A few years ago I baptized a man who had made a joyful profession of faith in Christ. Several months later he was living with a mistress. A friend and fellow member of our church appealed to him to obey God's Word and forsake his sin, but he refused. The friend then reminded this man of his recent baptism, during which he had made a public vow to live for Christ. To that he just laughed and said, "Get lost!"

The friend told me in deep grief about his encounter and asked, "How could this happen?" I, too, was pierced with sorrow to hear the news. But to offer my friend a word of consolation, I reminded him, "Even Jesus had His Judas."

Many people steer clear of the church because of its hypocrites. That shows the hypocrisy of those who stay away. Married life has its share of hypocrites, but that doesn't keep people from getting married. There are hypocrites in business, but that doesn't stop people from going into business. Society is filled with hypocrites of one kind or another, so why don't the people who say, "I can't stomach the church because of its hypocrisy" become a hermit? They have a double standard, and what is that but hypocrisy?

If a hypocrite is standing between you and Christ, then that person is closer to the Lord than you are. Charles Spurgeon once said, "The more a church flourishes, the more, I believe, do hypocrites get in, just as you see many a noxious creeping thing get into a garden after a shower of rain. The very things that make glad the flowers bring out these noxious things."[1]

So let's put away our excuses. Until Jesus returns, the church will always be contaminated with hypocrisy. We should be neither surprised nor repelled by it. What we should do is examine our own hearts. The example of Judas warns us that any Christian can prove to be a hypocrite. Every time we sing a hymn, put money in the offering plate, or tell others we are Christians, we give Jesus a kiss. Is it sincere? If not, we repeat Judas' sin by playing the hypocrite and betraying the Lord.

GREED DRIVES A WEDGE BETWEEN YOU AND CHRIST

For centuries scholars have theorized why Judas betrayed Jesus. Some have said that Judas, like Saul of Tarsus in Acts, became convinced that Jesus was a false Messiah. Others have claimed that Judas was offended by Jesus' seeming indifference to the law and violation of the Sabbath. Still others have theorized that Judas turned against Jesus because he was overlooked as the leader among the disciples. For example, Jesus took Peter, James, and John—but not Judas—to the Mount of Transfiguration (Mark 9:2). Nor did Judas get to sit next to Jesus at the Last Supper, as John did (John 13:23).

Thomas DeQuincey suggested that Judas's goal was not to get Jesus executed but to force Him to use His supernatural power. Just before giving Jesus the betrayal kiss, Judas said, "Hail, Rabbi!" (Matt. 26:49). By that he supposedly meant, "Unleash Your power and destroy these enemies of ours! Surely You would rather do that than have them arrest and crucify You!" But Judas was tragically mistaken.

We cannot, however, hold any of these theories with a firm grip, for the New Testament makes no efforts to delve into the psyche of Judas. What the text does say is that Judas gave in to the sin of greed. He "went to the chief priests, and said, 'What are you willing to give me to deliver Him up to you?' And they weighed out to him thirty pieces of silver. From then on he began looking for a good opportunity to betray Him" (vv. 14–16).

Judas is a classic example of the warning in 1 Timothy 6:10: "For the love of money is a root of all sorts of evil, and some by longing for it have wandered away from the faith, and pierced themselves with many a pang."

Today Jesus is still being sold out to the Devil. One person sells out for the price of a pornographic magazine. Another lets go of Christ for his or her weekly salary, which is earned by cheating business customers. Still another sells out Jesus in exchange for ungodly friends who would never associate with a Christian.

A pastor once boarded a bus and for his fare handed the driver a $10 bill. The driver counted out change for twenty dollars instead of ten. Thus, he gave the pastor $10 too much. At first the pastor thought to himself, *My, how God provides!* While riding along, he was rationalizing to himself how he needed the money more than the bus company. But that money began to trouble his conscience. As he stepped off the bus, the pastor held out the money to the driver and said, "Here, you made a mistake. You gave me too much change."

The driver smiled and said, "It was no mistake. I was in your church last Sunday and heard you preach against the love of money. When I saw you getting on the bus, I decided to see whether you really meant what you said."

Greed disguises itself and subtly tempts you to betray the one whom you call your Lord.

Sin Fails to Deliver on Its Promises

Matthew 27:3 reports that "when Judas, who had betrayed Him, saw that He had been condemned, he felt remorse and returned the thirty pieces of silver to the chief priests and elders." Underscore the words, "when Judas . . . saw." It wasn't until after he had committed the crime that he realized the enormity of his guilt. Before that, all he saw was the gain.

The words remind us of Adam and Eve. Consider what Scripture says after they ate the forbidden fruit in Eden: "Then the eyes of both of them were opened" (Gen. 3:7). Adam and Eve thought their disobedience to the divine command would make them like God. But after the damage was done, they saw differently. They realized that it only brought them shame. Just as with Judas, it promised them gain but delivered guilt.

We have experienced the same result, haven't we? Hebrews 3:13 warns us against "the deceitfulness of sin." It promises us life but brings death. It holds out the prospect of happiness, but in the end all we feel is misery. Sin is a liar. Judas bought the lie for thirty pieces of silver. Thus he showed, not just how much he thought Christ was worth, but how little he valued his own soul. As C. J. Wright has said:

> *Still, as of old,*
> *We by ourselves are priced;*
> *For thirty pieces Judas sold*
> *Himself, not Christ.*[2]

Many people have deserted their spouse to find happiness with someone else, only to discover later on that the wretchedness wasn't caused by their original partner, but by their own heart. They couldn't tolerate the monotony of a routine marriage. Dreams of a rapturous relationship with someone new enticed them. But the luster of the new relationship also faded to a drab routine, and sin had mocked another victim.

Whatever sin you might contemplate will not deliver on its promises. We tend to think of Judas as a cool, calculating, willing slave of Satan. But he was more like an insect that recklessly trespasses onto the spider's web. Don't assume you could never be a Judas. Just give Satan a foothold, and he will turn you into a traitor, too.

Remorse Is No Substitute for Repentance

Scripture tells us that after Judas betrayed Jesus, "he felt remorse and returned the thirty pieces of silver to the chief priests and elders, saying, 'I have sinned by betraying innocent blood'" (Matt. 27:3b–4a). What a tremendous confession! Judas didn't cop out by saying, "The devil made me do it" or "I didn't mean it." Nor did Judas try to shift the blame by claiming, "The chief priests paid me to hand Jesus over." Judas confessed, "I have sinned by betraying innocent blood." Judas was far from being the Devil incarnate. He was a man tortured by his dreadful mistake.

So there was hope for Judas, even after he proved untrue. If he had only taken his burden to Jesus, he would have found forgiveness. But he turned to the chief priests instead. Rather than give his sin to Jesus, Judas tried to return the money to the Savior's enemies. Judas tried to rid himself of guilt the human way rather than the divine way.

The human way to resolve guilt is through remorse, but God's way is through repentance. Second Corinthians 7:10 reveals the enormous difference between the two: "For the sorrow that is according to the will of God produces a repentance without regret, leading to salvation; but the sorrow of the world produces death." If Judas had repented, he would have been saved. But he stopped at remorse—worldly sorrow—and that produced physical, spiritual, and eternal death.

We must not look to our conscience to tell us the difference between right and wrong. Conscience tells us only to *do* the right thing. It doesn't show us what the right thing *is*. To learn these things, we must know God's Word. That's where Judas went wrong. He failed to take the scriptural course of action. He should have confessed his sin to Christ, but he resorted to people. Because they couldn't help him, his despair led him to take his own life.

When your conscience accuses you of doing something wrong, to whom do you go? A friend? A counselor? A pastor? They cannot solve your sin problem. Only Jesus can help you. He alone bore your sins when He died on the cross. And where did He take them? "As far as the east is from the west, so far has He removed our transgressions from us" (Ps. 103:12).

Action Steps

Scripture's last word on Judas is that after he committed suicide, he went "to his own place" (Acts 1:25). That's a veiled way of saying he went to hell. Rather than self-righteously despise Judas, let's understand that if it were not for God's grace, the destiny of Judas would also be ours. So let's confess:

> *Lord, when I read the traitor's doom,*
> *To his own place consigned,*
> *What holy fear and humble hope*
> *Together fill my mind!*

> *Traitor to You I too have been,*
> *But saved by matchless grace,*
> *Or else the lowest, hottest hell*
> *Had surely been my place.*[3]

I wonder what Jesus will say to Judas at the judgment. Maybe Christ will look into his eyes and ask, "Wasn't one death enough, Judas? I died for you so that you wouldn't have to be eternally punished. But you refused to trust in Me for forgiveness. You took your own life. Now you must also suffer the second death in hell."

Today Jesus says to you, "I died so that you won't have to." Do you rejoice at the thought of Him paying the price for your sins? Or, Judas-like, do you insist on punishing yourself with guilt and unnecessarily entering a Christless eternity? If you claim to have faith in Christ, prove it by repenting of your sins and enjoying the forgiveness of a loving heavenly Father.

Judas will always be remembered as the man who sold Jesus. You and I have also sold Jesus. But God has never sold His Son. He always gives Him freely. "The free gift of God is eternal life in Christ Jesus our Lord" (Rom. 6:23).

The opposite of selling Jesus is to accept Him by faith. And the opposite of betrayal is love. There is no middle ground between the two. Resolve to give Christ your faith and love. This is no trivial decision, for it determines whether you will spend eternity with Judas or with Jesus.

Study Guide

1. What do these passages teach about God's choice of us to be His people?

    *   Deuteronomy 7:7–8

    *   John 15:16

    *   1 Corinthians 1:27–29

    *   Ephesians 1:3–6

    *   2 Thessalonians 2:13

2. How could Judas live with Christ for three years and yet fail to be changed by Him?

3. According to each passage below, what change should take place in a Christian's life?

   • John 13:34–35

   • Romans 5:1

   • Ephesians 5:8

   • Philippians 4:6–8

   • 1 Thessalonians 5:18

   • 1 Peter 1:8

4. How do you know that Christ has brought about a genuine change of thinking and behavior in you?

5. Give an example of the way the Devil uses people today to destroy the work of Christ.

6. What are two or three telltale signs of a counterfeit Christian? Explain your answer.

7. How would you reply to someone who claims, "The church is full of hypocrites"?

8. Speaking of hypocrites, Jesus said, "You will know them by their fruits" (Matt. 7:16, 20). What do you think He meant by the word "fruits"?

9. Is there a difference between betraying Christ, as Judas did, and sinning against Him, as all Christians do? If so, what is the difference?

10. In what area of your life is Satan most likely to gain a foothold?

11. After betraying Christ, Judas took his own life (Matt. 27:5) and went "to his own place [hell]" (Acts 1:25). Is it possible to commit suicide and still enter heaven? Explain your answer. For help, compare Judges 16:30 with Hebrews 11:32.

12. How would you counsel a deeply depressed person who says, "I know I belong to Christ and am on my way to heaven, so I may as well take my own life"?

A DARING QUESTION:

"Which one of you convicts Me of sin?" (John 8:46)

TWO CHRISTIANS FOUND THEMSELVES arguing over whether it was possible to reach a state of perfection in this life. One challenged the other to name a single person in the Bible whose life showed no trace of sin.

"I can point to two of them," the friend claimed. He then opened his Bible to Luke 1:6 and read that Zacharias and his wife Elizabeth "were both righteous in the sight of God, walking blamelessly in all the commandments and requirements of the Lord."

"So do you consider yourself a believer like Zacharias?" asked the first man.

"Yes, I do!" retorted the second.

"Then you should read the rest of Luke 1, and you'll see that the angel Gabriel temporarily made Zacharias mute because of his unbelief!"

A person comes closest to perfection, according to the cynical saying, when filling out a job application form. But Jesus is the exception to the rule. When He asked "Which one of you convicts Me of sin?" (John 8:46), He was boldly claiming to be perfect. He was challenging His enemies to present evidence that He had ever done, said, or thought anything wrong. What a daring claim to make!

Try asking your spouse, "Can you prove me guilty of sin?" Ask it of your friends. Ask it of the people with whom you work. Let's face it. If we did that, we'd be cut down to size in a flash.

The Greek verb *elegchō,* which is rendered "convicts" in verse 46, means to "bring to light," "expose," or "set forth" something in order to reprove, correct, or show someone his or her fault.[1] Every Christian should understand the concept of conviction, for it is vital to our work of evangelism. Before we can lead people to Christ, they must come under the conviction of their sins. Their first step in getting saved and growing in Christlikeness is to understand that they are wicked.

THE MEANING OF CONVICTION

Our English verb *convict* means to "find or prove to be guilty" and to "convince of error or sinfulness." The related noun *conviction* refers to "the act or process of convicting of a crime, especially in a court of law."[2] When a defendant is convicted of a crime, the judge or jury renders a verdict of "guilty." Conviction goes beyond accusing someone of wrongdoing. The accusation must be proven.

The enemies of Christ accused Him of blasphemy, gluttony, drunkenness, breaking the Sabbath, and demon possession. But His question, "Which one of you convicts Me of sin?" (John 8:46), implies that they couldn't substantiate their claims. The NIV translates this verse, "Can any of you prove me guilty of sin?" No one in the crowd that day took Jesus up on His challenge. In the end their accusations were seen to be nothing more than hot air.

Conviction, then, is the Holy Spirit's work by which people become painfully aware in their conscience that they are guilty of sin before God, who is infinitely holy. Howard Cleveland describes it as "the work of the Holy Spirit by which the satanic blindness is lifted from men's eyes, and they are enabled to see themselves as they are in God's sight—guilty, defiled, and totally unable to save themselves."[3] Because Jesus was perfect, He never needed to be convicted of sin.

One summer afternoon a man I had never met entered my office. Visibly trembling, he confessed to me that he had stolen a car a week earlier. Since then, he had been unable to sleep and was heading for a nervous breakdown. Though he had spent twelve of his thirty-eight years in prison, he had never felt so conscience-stricken before. His one all-consuming passion was to return the car to its owner and relieve his guilty conscience.

I informed this man that his real problem was much deeper than grand larceny. He needed forgiveness for all his sins. He immediately agreed. I shared the good news of Christ with him, and together we knelt in prayer. He confessed his sins to God, asked for forgiveness, and trusted in Christ for salvation.

We then drove my car to a field in which he had stashed the stolen vehicle. After that he directed me to the owner's house. I explained to him where he could find his car, and interceded on behalf of the repentant thief. The owner was a Christian and agreed to forgive the offense and not seek prosecution.

That was seven years ago. Since then I have kept in touch with the converted thief, whose heart remains tender for Christ. Conviction did its work on him!

THE MESSAGE OF CONVICTION

Conviction carries with it a threefold message. First, it teaches us that *specific sins have separated us from God.* The man about whom I just spoke was broken down by the sin of theft. In Scripture, God convicted Joseph's brothers of selling him into slavery (Gen. 42:21), David of adultery and murder (Ps. 51), Isaiah of impure speech (Isa. 6:5), Zaccheus of extortion (Luke 19:8), and Peter of denying Christ (Luke 22:59–62). You may feel convicted of gossip, lying, cheating, lust, gluttony, or any number of specific sins.

According to John 16:8, the first issue about which the Spirit convicts people is sin. Many have a drinking problem but don't see it as a sin problem. To them it is a "chemical dependency" or an "addiction," not a personal sin against a holy God. People wrapped up in the sin of pride may feel good about their "positive self-image." A husband and wife who abort their baby may be persuaded that it was their "constitutional right," not an act of murder. Those who defy God's command to trust in Christ might excuse themselves by saying, "I'm just not cut out to be a Christian."

But conviction changes people's minds. It convinces them that these attitudes, actions, and lifestyles are sins. It casts a new light on the subject—the divine light. It unmasks specific thoughts, words, and acts and reveals their true nature as sins committed against a holy God.

Conviction's second message is that, *not just our sins, but also our sinfulness has separated us from God.* Conviction persuades us that we are corrupt to the core (Ps. 51:5; Jer. 17:9). Not just our thoughts, words, and actions, but also our hearts need changing. People under conviction know that making a few superficial changes in their life won't solve their sin problem. They won't settle for mere reformation; nothing less than a radical spiritual transformation is their goal (Rom. 12:1–2).

The third message of conviction is that *only Christ can solve our sin problem.* He alone can bring us forgiveness, make us spiritually brand-new, and reconcile us to the heavenly Father. God in His love does not leave us with no hope of being saved. When we are convicted with guilt, He offers us the good news of Christ—that He was punished for us on a cross so that we might go free.

Think about a boy and his kite. He has let out the string so far that he can't see the kite anymore. Someone comes along and inquires, "What have you got up there?"

"A kite," the boy answers.

104 13 Crucial Questions Jesus Wants to Ask You

"How do you know the kite is still up there when you can't see it?" the person asks.

"Because," the boy answers, "I can feel it pulling on me."

Conviction is like that kite. It is the upward and invisible pull of God. With a force far greater than a string, it pulls us, not down into the pit of despair, but up to spiritual freedom in Christ. Often the pull is painful, but its purpose is to save us from eternal destruction.

Someone once complained to evangelist Billy Sunday that his preaching was too convicting to people's consciences. "You rub the cat's fur the wrong direction," he was told.

Sunday's reply was just as convicting as his preaching: "Then tell the cat to turn around!"

That's what God says in conviction. "Turn away from your sin and turn toward My Son, Jesus!" Apart from Him we are living in a backwards, unnatural condition.

Charles Spurgeon's testimony about his own conviction reveals how God takes the heart He has broken and heals it in Christ:

> My heart was fallow and covered with weeds, but on a certain day the great Farmer came and began to plow my soul. Ten black horses were his team, and it was a sharp plowshare that he used, and the plowers made deep furrows. The Ten Commandments were those black horses, and the justice of God, like a plowshare, tore my spirit. I was condemned, undone, destroyed, lost, helpless, hopeless. I thought hell was before me. But after the plowing came the sowing. God, who plowed the heart in mercy, made it conscious that it needed the gospel, and then the gospel seed was joyfully received.[4]

THE MASTER OF CONVICTION

There is only one person who can convict people of their need for Christ; it is the Holy Spirit. With Him in mind, Jesus declared in John 16:8, "And He, when He comes, will convict the world concerning sin, and righteousness, and judgment."

Trying to convict people of their sins apart from the ministry of the Spirit is like telling a corpse to stand up. Even if you preach the gospel to unbelievers, if God's Spirit is not speaking through you, it is like playing classical music into the ears of a deaf person.

Some Christians fondly remember how they were converted through the preaching of a specific sermon by a fiery evangelist. *If only my hus-*

band could hear that sermon by that same evangelist, a woman imagines, *I just know he will give his life to Christ!*

Don't be so sure. It wasn't that evangelist or his sermon that brought you under a burden of guilt and led you to the Lord. It was the Spirit. No doubt on the same day you were converted others were present who remained in their unbelief. So who's to say your husband wouldn't follow their example rather than yours if he could hear that evangelist preach?

The Holy Spirit is the master of conviction. When Peter preached about Christ on the Day of Pentecost, three thousand listeners were "pierced to the heart" (Acts 2:37). Some time later the apostles spoke about Christ to the Jewish Supreme Court, and again "they were cut to the quick" (5:33). When Stephen, the first recorded Christian martyr, preached about Christ, his hearers also were "cut to the quick" (7:54).

Not even an apostle could pierce people to the heart. And no human being can cut people to the quick. This is a ministry that only the Spirit can accomplish. When unbelievers build a wall of defense against your witness, be encouraged, for the master of conviction can pierce it! So don't give up! Be available for Him to use to show people their need to trust in Christ.

THE MEANS OF CONVICTION

We find in the Bible three means through which the Spirit brings people to a knowledge of their sinful condition. The first is *the Word of God.* Hebrews 4:12 says, "For the word of God is living and active and sharper than any two-edged sword, and piercing as far as the division of soul and spirit, of both joints and marrow, and able to judge the thoughts and intentions of the heart."

One of the greatest movements of the Spirit recorded in the Old Testament occurred in the ancient city of Nineveh, whose population was about 120,000 (Jonah 4:11).[5] God told Jonah to declare "the proclamation which I am going to tell you" (3:2). It was only a brief message: "Yet forty days and Nineveh will be overthrown" (v. 4). When Nineveh's king heard it, he trembled in fear, repented of his sins, and believed in God. So did all of Nineveh's citizens, "from the greatest to the least of them" (v. 5). Jonah preached God's message verbatim, and the entire city came under the Spirit's conviction!

Today God continues to convict people through the preaching of His Word:

> *My pastor shapes his sermons*
> *From A to final Z*
> *In clear and forthright language,*
> *And aims them straight at me.*

And when he gets to preaching,
I look around to see
If there might be another
Deserving more than me.

But every soul looks saintly,
Their hearts to heaven turn,
While I, in my conviction,
Can only sit and squirm.

You know, I often wonder,
If I should miss a day,
Would he without his target
Have anything to say?

—author unknown

Some time ago a woman told me she was sexually involved with a man other than her husband. I asked her whether she regretted it, and she said no. Nor did she think it was wrong. "I love my boyfriend," she explained, "and besides, my marriage has been dead for a long time."

I took my Bible and read passages to her that said she was committing the sin of adultery. I made no comments and gave no interpretations; I merely allowed Scripture to speak for itself. Immediately she broke down and began to cry.

I assured her that Christ was willing to forgive her. She replied, "I'd like to take Him up on that." I warned her that she had to break off the relationship with her boyfriend and recommit herself to her husband and the Lord. When she promised to do that, I knew she was serious. In the next few minutes she trusted in Christ for salvation. God's Word convicted her! It compelled her to agree with the Lord that she was sinning and to turn to Christ in faith for forgiveness.

Second, *the Spirit uses the witness of Christians to convict unbelievers of their sin and their need to trust in Jesus.* Bill Bright, the founder of Campus Crusade for Christ, tells a story of an encounter he had with a philosophy major at the University of Houston:

> Our campus director invited Benjamin to visit with me at the coffee shop after a long day of meetings, and Benjamin welcomed the opportunity to "debate another religious fanatic." The three of us visited for more than an hour, but it seemed like a classic case of noncommunication. Benjamin would give lengthy quotes from atheistic philosophers, and when he stopped for

breath I would tell him that God loves him and offers a wonderful plan for his life. He would then state that God didn't exist, and I would reply that I had felt pretty much the same way when I was an agnostic, but Jesus had changed my life. I had been up and running since before dawn, so I was exhausted. It didn't seem like the conversation was going anywhere and I suggested we call it a night. "Would you mind dropping me off at my dorm?" Benjamin asked us. I got in the back seat, thinking I'd get a start on some much-needed sleep. But before we pulled out of the driveway, Benjamin turned around in the front passenger's seat and said, "Mr. Bright, everything you said tonight hit me in the heart. And I'd like to receive Christ right now."

Needless to say, sleep suddenly lost its importance. Benjamin had given no indication that he was close to accepting the claims of Christ. There had been no positive response during our awkward conversation. I hadn't been what you'd call profound in my verbal witness. But the Holy Spirit had prepared Benjamin's heart, and had used me in spite of my weariness to penetrate his facade and communicate God's love.[6]

Third, *God's Spirit convicts people through our prayers.* As Jesus was dying on the cross, He prayed, "Father, forgive them; for they do not know what they are doing" (Luke 23:34). The result was that before leaving the cross that afternoon, all the guards confessed, "Truly this was the Son of God!" (Matt. 27:54), and all the spectators beat their breasts (Luke 23:48), for the hatred of their hearts had led to the execution of Jesus. Some time later 3,000 Jews—some of whom doubtless called out for Jesus' crucifixion—were converted (Acts 2:41). In response to Jesus' prayer, God convicted some of His murderers!

Stephen's last words during his stoning were, "Lord, do not hold this sin against them!" (Acts 7:60). Some time later, Saul, who had conspired to murder Stephen, trusted in Christ, got saved, and became one of His apostles. Centuries ago Augustine remarked, "If Stephen had not prayed, the church would not have had the apostle Paul."

Surely you know people who need to be under the conviction of the Spirit and are not. Pray for them! Perhaps God has not pierced their hearts because you have not pleaded with yours before Him in prayer.

A friend of mine is the pastor of a rapidly growing church. Newcomers flock to it, trust in Christ for salvation, and become responsible church members. Someone asked my friend the secret of his church's growth. He answered in one word: "Prayer." That's your secret, too. Prayer is the key that opens hearts that are locked tight against Christ.

Action Steps

Here are three godly steps you can take in response to Jesus' crucial question about conviction. First, choose to believe that conviction, though painful, is nothing to fear. Those who do fear it can stifle it up to a point. The same Jews who were pierced to the heart by Stephen's sermon were first described as "stiff-necked" and "always resisting the Holy Spirit" (Acts 7:51). They had smothered the convicting fire of God's Spirit in their hearts.

Is that what you're doing? I heard about a man who purchased a microscope, brought it home, and thoroughly enjoyed using it—until one night when he examined the food he was about to eat for dinner. He was aghast to find tiny creatures crawling in it. So what did he do? He smashed the microscope!

In a similar way, many people respond wrongly when conviction enables them to see their sins for the first time. They turn *away* from Christ rather than *to* Him. The pain of guilt is so acute, they flee from it. But pain is a gift from God. It tells us to take our hands away from the hot stove. If we didn't feel pain, our hands would burn to a crisp.

And so with the spiritual pain of conviction. Its aim is to save us from the agony of condemnation. Jesus promised, "I did not come to judge the world, but to save the world" (John 12:47). Thus, His question, "Which one of you convicts Me of sin?" was meant, not to threaten us with judgment, but to spare us of it by driving us to believe in Him as our perfect Savior.

So don't fear conviction! It's only when you writhe under a deep sense of sin that you rejoice over a great salvation. Jesus never looked so beautiful as against the background of your own wickedness.

Second, ask God, "Have I been entertaining a sin in my life for which You want to pierce my heart?" Scripture declares, "There is not a single man in all the earth who is always good and never sins" (Eccl. 7:20 LB). So until we step into heaven, even we Christians on occasion will need to have the guilt of our sins brought home to our hearts. Think of this as spiritual growing pains. Maybe God wants to convict you of an unforgiving spirit, a fiery temper, a secret lust, a preoccupation with pleasure, or a lack of love for a fellow Christian. If you're an unbeliever, God wants you to feel uneasy with your rejection of Christ. There is no sin worse than that.

What if you honestly don't feel any conviction? What if your heart is so hard that you are unable to grieve over your sins? That leads to our third action step: Even then trust in Christ for salvation. If you can't come to Him *with* a heart broken over sin, then come to Him *for* it. If you feel no natural sorrow for your sins, approach Jesus and trust Him to teach you supernaturally to grieve over the many ways you have caused Him to grieve. When you come to Christ, not because you have something to offer Him but because He has everything to offer you, you give solid evidence that conviction has begun its good work in you.

Study Guide

1. Define or describe the conviction of sin.

2. Each of the following verses suggests a reason people should feel conviction. What are these reasons?

   • Isaiah 53:6

   • Isaiah 64:6

   • Romans 3:23

   • 1 John 3:4

3. Share an experience in which God convicted you of sin, either at your conversion or in Christian experience.

4. Must all people feel the conviction of sin before they can become Christians, or can they simply trust in Christ for salvation without feeling sin's guilt? Explain your answer.

5. Acts 7:51 implies that the Spirit's conviction can be resisted to a point. In each verse below, who admitted, "I have sinned"? Was the confession genuine or insincere? Explain your answers.

    • Exodus 9:27

    • Numbers 22:34

    • Joshua 7:20

    • 1 Samuel 26:21

    • 2 Samuel 12:13

    • Matthew 27:3–4

    • Luke 15:18, 21

6. Does the Spirit convict people irresistibly, so that they are unable to reject Christ? Does God ever make people believe against their will? Explain your answer.

7. In John 16:7–11 what does it mean that the Spirit will "convict the world concerning sin, and righteousness, and judgment"? Check other versions for help in understanding this passage.

8. Does Satan try to convict you of sin? How does his goal differ from God's?

A CHALLENGING QUESTION:

"Do you believe this?"
(John 11:26)

AFTER HE STEPPED DOWN FROM office as President of the United States, Thomas Jefferson took up the personal project of rewriting the New Testament. He believed in Jesus as merely a good moral teacher. Jefferson excised the miracles in an attempt to discover Jesus' "real message." The final words of the gospel story in his New Testament were, "There laid they Jesus, and rolled a great stone to the door of the sepulcher and departed." Thomas Jefferson didn't believe in the resurrection power of Christ.

In John 11:25–26, Jesus reassured Martha, who was grieving over the death of her brother Lazarus, "I am the resurrection and the life; he who believes in Me shall live even if he dies, and everyone who lives and believes in Me shall never die." This is perhaps the most startling of the eight "I am" statements of Jesus recorded in John's gospel.

Many times I've heard these words repeated by pastors at funerals. But I do not remember ever hearing them quote the end of verse 26, where Jesus asked Martha, "Do you believe this?" Our Lord wants us to believe the same things He asked Martha to believe. His previous statement includes five articles of faith.

DO YOU BELIEVE JESUS CONQUERED DEATH?

Perhaps with tears streaming down her face, Martha had said to Jesus a little earlier, "Lord, if You had been here, my brother would not have died" (v. 21). Jesus reassured her that Lazarus would rise again (v. 23), but Martha accepted His promise as only a doctrinal platitude that had little or no relevance to her present grief. Perhaps she nodded her head as she agreed that her brother would rise again in the resurrection of the last day (v. 24). At that point our Lord stated, "I am the resurrection and the life" (v. 25). He did not say, "I raise people from the dead" or even "I will rise from the dead." His words were much more forceful.

In my earliest years as a pastor, a member of the church and I visited in the home of a skeptic. When he learned that we were from the church, he proudly informed us that he could put no faith in Christ, because all religions were the same. We shared our personal testimonies of what Christ meant to us, explained to him the plan of salvation, and invited him to our church. But he remained unmoved. He was not hostile. He merely complained that, with all the many religions in the world, he couldn't possibly know which was true. He even said it was presumptuous of us to place Jesus in a class by Himself among all the religious founders.

As we were saying good night at the door, my friend made a parting remark: "Sir, just remember this. Christianity is the only religion whose founder is still alive, because Jesus Christ is the one person who came back from the dead." The reflective silence of the man who earlier had offered excuses galore shouted back to us that he was beginning to see the light.

Buddha, Confucius, Muhammad, Joseph Smith, Charles Taze Russell, Mary Baker Eddy, and all the other religious founders are dead. Christ lives on. There may be comparable religions, but Christianity is not one of them. It is incomparable, for only Jesus conquered death.

The Bible confirms this truth in several ways. First, Jesus restored three people to life, each in a different setting. He brought back the twelve-year-old daughter of Jairus *before* her funeral (Mark 5:35–43), a widow's only son *during* his funeral (Luke 7:11–17), and Lazarus four days *after* his funeral (John 11:11–44). From these incidents we see that nothing is too hard for Jesus, for He is the resurrection and the life.

Jesus' healing ministry also confirms the truth of His messianic claim. He restored sight to dead eyes, hearing to dead ears, and strength to dead limbs. Everything Jesus touched was healed, for He is the resurrection and the life.

Jesus' own resurrection also marks Him out as the Conqueror of death and the Lord of life. Because He is God, He had to rise from the dead, for "death no longer is master over Him" (Rom. 6:9). When He was resurrected, He demonstrated that He is the immortal and eternal God. In light of this, it is truly amazing that He ever experienced death in the first place (Heb. 2:9, 14–15).

We can also confirm Jesus' claim about being the resurrection and the life in the lives of countless believers. Christians are people whose hearts were once dead toward God, but Jesus gave them life (Eph. 2:4–5). Ask any disciple whether Jesus is the resurrection and the life. He or she will tell you, "I'm convinced that He is, for He gave *me* new life!"

Not only does Jesus resurrect our hearts from the graveyard of sin, but He also restores life to dead marriages, dead families, and dead hopes. Everything He gets involved with turns to life, for He is the conqueror of death. Do you believe this?

Do You Believe Jesus Makes Life Worth Living?

Our Lord told Martha on that sorrowful occasion, "I am . . . the life" (John 11:25). He didn't limit His claim to *giving* life, *showing* life, or *teaching* about life. He asserted that He *is* life itself. Again in John 14:6, Jesus affirmed, "I am . . . the life." And Colossians 3:4 speaks of "Christ, who is our life."

Put simply, we can say that Jesus makes life worth living. Millions of people need to hear this good news. In the United States, suicides have doubled among teenagers and young adults in the last ten years. Half a million people attempt suicide every year. For every twenty murders in our country, there are twenty-five suicides. In Los Angeles, more people take their own lives than die in traffic accidents. Eighty percent of suicide victims have attempted it previously.

William Coleman wrote, "Each Sunday most ministers have several people in their congregations who are high risks to attempt suicide. On casual acquaintance these people seem little different from non-suicidal people. . . . Probably 90 percent of the population will consider it as a possibility sometime in their lives."[1]

Rod was a friend of mine with whom I worked one summer at a Christian camp during our late teenage years. He knew the Lord but always spoke about how meaningless life was. He was virtually obsessed with heaven, which is quite unusual for a teenager. Constantly he spoke about his desire to leave this earth and find his joy in the presence of the Lord.

A few months later I heard that a truck had struck the side of a car in which Rod had been a passenger. The car's driver escaped injury, but Rod died on impact. Those of us who knew him couldn't help but feel that God had given Rod his heart's desire. When he despaired of life, the Lord took it from him.

Life can be a pressure cooker. Sometimes you become stretched to the limit. But if Jesus Christ lives in you, He can give you joy even in the most distressing of situations. He always makes life worth living. Do you believe this?

Do You Believe Death Is Not Final?

Jesus said to Martha, "He who believes in Me shall live even if he dies" (John 11:25). Often we look at death as the end of life, but here our Lord reassures us that death does not have the last word. Death is still a reality, but Jesus transcends it. If we belong to Him by faith, we can look forward to spiritual life beyond the grave and to a physical resurrection when He returns.

Several years ago I attended the funeral of a woman who had led a brilliant Christian life. At the graveside her pastor said, "Julia isn't dead! She didn't really die!" He was trying to comfort the family and friends with the thought that Julia was in the presence of her Lord, but I think he went too far. In verse 25, Jesus Himself said that the believer "dies." Our Lord didn't deny death; rather, He offered hope that went beyond it.

Instead of claiming, "Julia isn't dead! She didn't really die!" her pastor could have said, "Julia is dead physically. But the real Julia continues to live with Christ in heaven. And at Jesus' second coming, He will open up this grave and restore even her body to life."

A tombstone of a man named Peas bears this inscription:

> *Here lies the body of old man Peas,*
> *Beneath the daisies and the trees.*
> *But Peas ain't here, only the pod,*
> *For Peas shelled out and is gone to God!*

Since death is not final for the Christian, we shouldn't cling to this earthly life as if it were the most precious thing we possess. Many times I've visited Christians in hospitals who can think only about physical health, though they are well advanced in years and on the brink of death. I would like to say to them, "Isn't it wonderful to think that in a few days you'll be home with your Lord in heaven?" But all they can talk about is regaining their health and returning to their earthly home. Many believers put far too much stock in the physical body. You would think that death brought everything to an end and that we had no afterlife to look forward to.

We can apply Jesus' words to more than just physical death. Many people are dead to the hurts and needs of others. Some husbands and wives are dead to the feelings of their mates. Such deadness need not be permanent. I can imagine Jesus promising, "If you believe in Me, I'll bring you back from the death of your present life." Do you believe this?

Do You Believe Faith in Christ Divides Humanity?

Jesus didn't promise everyone life beyond the grave. He offered this sure hope only to the person "who believes in Me" (v. 25). Jesus did not say, "Those who attend church or who live good lives will live even if they die."

Faith alone brings salvation. And not just any faith. Our Lord did not say, "Anyone who believes in God as a Creator . . ." or "Anyone who believes in the Bible . . ." or even "Anyone who believes certain things about Me will live even if they die." The condition was, "He who believes in Me."

Suppose you are driving your car toward an intersection where the traffic light is red. You put your foot on the brake, only to push it to the floor with absolutely no resistance. You pump the pedal again and again, but nothing happens. The brake fluid has leaked out, and you plow into a car that is waiting at the intersection.

Later you fix the leak, add new brake fluid, and then drive toward that same intersection. Again the light is red. With fear and trembling because of your previous experience, you step on the brake. This time you feel a firm pedal under your foot. You had strong faith in the brake when it failed and weak faith when it worked. Even strong faith, if it has no worthy object, is useless. But weak faith, placed in the right object, will be blessed. What matters is not strong faith, but faith in a strong object.

Jesus alone is that strong object. If your faith rests in anything or anyone other than Him, it will accomplish nothing. We can divide humanity into two basic groups: those who believe in Christ and those who don't. This issue determines whether you will enjoy eternity in heaven or be banished to hell. Faith in Christ makes all the difference in this life and the next. Do you believe this?

DO YOU BELIEVE CHRISTIANS NEED NOT FEAR DEATH?

Jesus' next words to Martha progressed a step beyond His promises up to this point: "Everyone who lives and believes in Me shall never die" (v. 26). The Greek phrase rendered "shall never die" is forceful in the original and could be translated "in no way will die." This should not be understood in a physical sense, for Christians die every day. Rather, Jesus is declaring that believers will live spiritually and eternally with Him in heaven, as He described in John 14:1–3. In the most emphatic terms He is saying that believers need not fear what lies beyond death.

Many people, for all practical purposes, have outlawed the subject of death. They regard it as unmentionable. They shield their children from thoughts of it. They shudder at the idea of attending a funeral. Many pastors who conduct funerals gloss over the seriousness of preparing for death. Why? Because people are afraid to die.

The Russian writer Fyodor Dostoyevsky (1821–1881) was convicted of sedition and sentenced to death. He was standing before the firing squad when the order saving his life arrived. "The certainty of inescapable death and the uncertainty of what is to follow are the most dreadful anguish in the world," he later wrote of his experience.[2]

People who have not trusted in Christ for salvation have good reason to fear death, for they're only a heartbeat away from hell. Once people go there, they cannot return (Heb. 9:27). Hell is a place of eternal misery, pain, darkness, despair, weeping, and gnashing of teeth (Rev. 20:11–15).

But Scripture describes the Christian's experience of death in much different terms. It is a carrying away by angels (Luke 16:22), a trip to Paradise (23:43), a move into the heavenly Father's house (John 14:2), life in the presence of Christ (2 Cor. 5:8), a gain (Phil. 1:21), and a departure to a much better place (v. 23).

A Christian man with a brief time to live was afraid of dying. He confided in a fellow believer, who didn't know how to comfort him. Suddenly a scratching was heard at the door. The friend opened it, and in bounded his dog. The dog had followed him down the street to the dying man's house. The dog wagged its tail and licked its master's face, obviously glad to be with him.

"My dog has never been in your house before, so it didn't know what it was like in here," the dog's owner told his dying friend. "But knowing I was here, the animal entered the unfamiliar house with confidence. Death is unknown territory to you, but you can be sure that your Savior is waiting for you on the other side. When you pass through that door, He will welcome you. That's all you need to know."

Is that all you need to know? When Paul thought about death, he wrote, "We are of good courage" (2 Cor. 5:8). Because his faith was in Christ, he had no reason to fear death. Do you believe this?

Action Steps

Doubting the promises of Christ is no casual matter. Instead, it is the ultimate insult to a loving Lord. Therefore, as a first step in answering Jesus' question, ask Him to make you a person marked by faith. Ever since Eden, the human race has disbelieved the words of God. The Lord warned Adam, "In the day that you eat from [the tree of the knowledge of good and evil] you shall surely die" (Gen. 2:17). Later the Devil came along and contradicted that statement. He promised Eve, "You surely shall not die!" (Gen. 3:4). At that moment Eve had a decision to make: "Will I believe what God has said or what Satan says?"

Each of us faces those same two alternatives. Jesus has claimed to be the conqueror of death and the Lord of life—both temporal and eternal. He asks, "Do you believe this?" There is no middle ground. If you don't say, "Yes, Lord, I believe You are everything You claim to be," you will be saying by default to the Devil, "I believe you."

Jesus' question is not, "Do you feel good when you stand at the grave of a loved one?" Christ wept at the tomb of Lazarus on the same day that He spoke to Martha (John 11:35). He knows firsthand the heartache you feel when you attend a family member's funeral. The issue is not feelings, but faith. Feelings are untrustworthy and temporary, whereas faith in Christ is reliable and enduring.

Yes, you grieve when a loved one dies. But do you believe that Jesus is the ultimate conqueror of death? Like everyone else, you are sometimes bombarded with trials and problems. But do you believe that Christ makes life worth living in spite of them? When a Christian passes away, a real separation takes place. Often it brings loneliness into your life. But do you believe that your loneliness will not last forever, that someday you will be reunited? Granted, death holds some mysteries. But do you believe that your Lord and Savior is waiting to welcome you home?

What if you don't believe Jesus' promises? Then the opposite of what He said to Martha applies to you: "He who does not believe in Me shall surely die even though he lives, and everyone who dies without believing in Me will never see the light of heaven." Can you be content with that as your epitaph? If not, take Christ at His word. He would never deceive you.

Perhaps you can say, "I've already settled the matter of faith in Christ. I do believe all these things!" Then let the whole world know. If Christ is your resurrection, prove it by showing others the new quality of life He has given you. If Christ is your life, demonstrate it by living in dedication to Him. Because He showered you with an unparalleled love, vow that your love for Him will also be unrivaled. Genuine faith says, "Yes, Lord, I believe this!" Then it lives what it claims to believe.

Study Guide

1. Because Jesus is the resurrection and the life, His followers should show evidence of their salvation by a newness of life that He has given them. Second Corinthians 5:17 speaks about this new life. In what specific ways can this verse be put into practice in your life?

2. David's words in 1 Samuel 20:3 are true of every human being: "There is hardly a step between me and death." If you should die today, are you certain you would spend eternity with Christ? If so, why?

3. When the Thessalonian Christians sorrowed over their loved ones who had died, Paul said he did not want them to "grieve like the rest of men, who have no hope" (1 Thess. 4:13 NIV). What is this great hope? How does it help believers in Christ to grieve differently from nonbelievers?

4. Summarize what these verses teach about Christian hope:

    • Romans 5:5

    • Colossians 1:27

    • 1 Timothy 1:1

    • Titus 2:13

    • Hebrews 6:18–19

    • 1 Peter 1:3

5. Jesus promised life beyond the grave to the person "who believes in Me" (John 11:25). How would you explain to a unsaved inquirer what it means to trust in Christ?

6. What do these passages teach about faith?

    • Romans 5:1

    • Romans 10:17

    • Romans 14:23

    • 1 Corinthians 2:5

    • 1 Corinthians 13:2

    • 1 Corinthians 15:17

    • 2 Corinthians 5:7

    • Galatians 5:6

    • Ephesians 2:8–9

    • Ephesians 6:16

    • Philippians 3:9

    • Hebrews 11:1

    • Hebrews 11:6

7. Why do you think even some Christians fear death?

8. Share your own experience of being separated from someone you loved who has died. How did that person's faith or lack of faith in Christ affect your grief?

9. What are your own thoughts about death and life beyond the grave?

10. What area of your life that seems to be dead (for example, your faith, hope, marriage, or relationship with a child) would you like Jesus to "resurrect"?

12

A CHILLING QUESTION:

"Will you lay down your life for Me?" (John 13:38)

WORLD MISSIONS EXPERT David Barrett, editor of the *World Christian Encyclopedia,* estimated that 330,000 Christians were martyred in 1990. According to Barrett, one of every 200 missionaries, pastors, and evangelists is killed in some regions. This trend, he says, is likely to become worse. His estimate, a decade before the end of the century, was that in the year 2000 half a million Christians would be martyred for their faith.

Daniel Kyanda, who narrowly escaped execution under Idi Amin in Uganda, now represents Christian Solidarity International in Nairobi, Kenya. He conducts seminars throughout Africa on preparing for persecution because "when I see more and more Africans being converted, I just conclude that each one is a candidate for persecution."[1]

In John 13:37, Peter boasted to Jesus, "I will lay down my life for You." Immediately the Lord challenged His disciple with this question: "Will you lay down your life for Me?" Jesus prophesied that on that very night a rooster "shall not crow, until you deny Me three times" (v. 38).

Peter's example teaches us that, in general, people who brag about their commitment to Christ are the least committed.

Would you lay down your life for Christ? You might reply, "How can I possibly know until the time comes?" Good question. Still, we should not wait until the secret police knock on our door before we consider our response to the possibility of martyrdom. Jesus' question to Peter does not caution us not to prepare for such a prospect. We should avoid only a rash presumption of courage.

Imagine making last good-byes to your spouse and children before being executed as a Christian. Tears stream down their faces. Their arms are stretched out to you. Their voices plead, "Don't leave us. We need you!" Would you tell them, "My greater loyalty is to Christ; I must die for Him rather than disown Him"? Martyrdom is the kind of possibility that should inspire awe in every believer.

MANY HAVE BEEN WILLING TO DIE FOR CHRIST

Many believers whose stories are recorded in the Bible put their lives on the line for their Lord. In Genesis 22, God tested Abraham's faith and obedience by commanding him to offer his son, Isaac, as a burnt offering. The patriarch passed his test, for the Lord didn't restrain him until his knife was about to plunge toward Isaac.

It's fascinating that we do not read that Isaac questioned his father. While Abraham tied his son to the altar, Isaac didn't shout, "Dad, what are you doing? Have you lost your mind?" Nor did he try to strike a deal for his release. Isaac was willing to die for the Lord who had guided his father to that point. As a result, Isaac stands out in Scripture as a type of Christ, who obeyed His heavenly Father to the point of death on a cross.

Queen Esther was made of martyrs' stuff. Her cousin Mordecai told her about a plot to exterminate the Jewish people and begged her to intercede with her husband, King Ahasuerus. But it was against the law for her even to approach him uninvited. Esther said she would take the chance, and, "If I perish, I perish" (Esther 4:16). After three days of fasting by the Jews, she sought the king's presence (5:1). Revealing to him her own identity as a Jew, she exposed herself as a target of the planned massacre. She demonstrated through her words and actions her willingness to lay down her life for Yahweh, the God of the Jews.

In the Book of Daniel, Shadrach, Meshach, and Abednego refused to worship King Nebuchadnezzar's golden image when threatened with a blazing death in a furnace. They replied, "If it be so, our God whom we serve is able to deliver us from the furnace of blazing fire; and He will deliver us out of your hand, O king. But even if He does not, let it be known to you, O king, that we are not going to serve your gods or worship the golden image that you have set up" (Dan. 3:17–18).

That was all Nebuchadnezzar needed to hear. He immediately gave orders for the furnace to be heated seven times hotter than usual and for the three defiant Jews to be bound and thrown into the blazing inferno (vv. 19–20). Without so much as a whimper they went into the flames (v. 21), ready to burn to death for their belief. And the Lord delivered them (vv. 22–27). Nebuchadnezzar afterward wondered at those who "were willing to give up their lives rather than serve or worship any god except their own God" (v. 28b NIV).

When ordered not to pray to anyone—whether divine or human—

except King Darius for thirty days, Daniel's relationship with the Lord remained inviolable. When arrested for praying to Yahweh, he didn't flinch at the prospect of being thrown to the lions. And he had no assurance that the Lord would protect him. Daniel was willing to die (Dan. 6).

John the Baptist knew all too well that confronting Herod's adulterous relationship could cost him his life, and it did. John's faith in a God of righteousness and holiness compelled him to pay the dreadful price (Mark 6:17–29).

After preaching his convicting sermon in Acts 7, Stephen took the truth of Christ all the way to a martyr's death.

The Spirit disclosed to Paul that bonds and affliction awaited him in every city to which he would bring the gospel. Hearing that, the apostle testified, "But I do not consider my life of any account as dear to myself, in order that I may finish my course, and the ministry which I received from the Lord Jesus, to testify solemnly of the gospel of the grace of God" (Acts 20:24). He described his upcoming death at the hands of the Roman government as "being poured out as a drink offering" (2 Tim. 4:6).

Scripture also speaks of unnamed heroes of the faith who were stoned, sawn in two, or run through with a sword (Heb. 11:37).

Church history is studded with examples of believers who laid down their lives for Christ. Around A.D. 117, Ignatius of Antioch, an elderly church leader, was taken to Rome under military guard to be mauled by savage beasts in the Colosseum. At nearly every stop along the way he penned letters to various churches. In one of them he described himself as "the wheat of God ground by the teeth of wild animals, that I may be found the pure bread of God." After facing the jeers of the emperor and the condemnation of the crowd, the lions were turned loose on him. Ignatius thrust his arm into a lion's mouth, and as his bones cracked, he shouted, "Now I begin to be a Christian!"[2]

During one of the last Roman persecutions, all believers in Christ were ordered to renounce their faith in Him or be put to death. Forty soldiers of the Twelfth Legion, stationed at Sebaste in Armenia, refused. They were stripped naked, forced out on a frozen lake, and left to die. To tempt them to apostatize, fires and warm baths were prepared on the bank. But the forty braced themselves by chanting together this prayer: "O Lord, forty wrestlers have come forth to fight for Thee. Grant that forty wrestlers may gain the victory!"

Finally, one man could bear the suffering no longer. He walked off the lake, renounced the Lord Jesus, and was cared for by the Roman guards. Out on the lake the chant was heard again: "O Lord, forty wrestlers have come forth to fight for Thee. Grant that forty wrestlers may gain the victory!"

Their prayer was answered when one of the guards, Sempronius, was moved to the point of conversion as he witnessed the faithfulness of the thirty-nine. He declared himself a Christian, stripped off his clothes, and took the place of the defector. Once again the chant resumed: "O Lord, forty wrestlers have come forth to fight for Thee. Grant that forty wrestlers may gain the victory!" Hours later most of the forty had frozen to death. The others were executed. All gained the victory for which they had prayed.[3]

What would you do in situations like that? Do you have a faith worth dying for? I can imagine Jesus asking us, "Will you lay down your life for Me?" (John 13:38).

JESUS DEMANDS THAT HIS DISCIPLES BE WILLING TO DIE FOR HIM

In Matthew 16:24, our Lord laid out three nonnegotiables for all who would follow Him: "If any one wishes to come after Me, let him deny himself, and take up his cross, and follow Me." The three Greek verbs used in the last part of this verse are imperatives, absolute commands that must be obeyed. These same three requirements for discipleship are repeated in the parallel passages of Mark 8:34 and Luke 9:23.

Consider that second imperative: What does it mean to take up your cross? In its simplest form, it refers to a willingness to die for Christ. Many Christians overlook this key truth. People say, "My cross is a grouchy mother-in-law" or "I bear the cross of arthritis pain." When Jesus tells us to take up our cross, He implies that it is something we can choose not to do. We can do little about a grouchy mother-in-law or arthritis pain, whatever our level of commitment to Christ. But the cross is something we deliberately accept that we could otherwise turn down.

In Jesus' day, crosses were used for one purpose—to execute people. To take up our cross, therefore, is to say to Christ, "I am willing to lay down my life for You." In his commentary on Mark's gospel, H. B. Swete wrote that to take up the cross is to "put oneself into the position of a condemned man on his way to execution."[4]

The people to whom Jesus originally spoke these words recorded in Matthew 16:24 undoubtedly had seen condemned criminals take up crosses. These cross-bearers were not exercising to lose a couple of unwanted pounds. They were on a one-way trip to a hideous and agonizing death. In the first century A.D., believers who took up their crosses proved their ultimate commitment to Christ. There was no such thing as partial crucifixion. They were leaving everything behind and going the limit for their Lord.

In the mid-1950s, Jim Elliot and Pete Fleming were young men who sensed a call from God to serve as missionaries to the Auca Indians in Ecuador. While a student in college, Jim wrote, "I'm ready to die for the salvation of the Aucas. He is no fool who gives what he cannot keep to gain what he cannot lose."

About that same time, Pete Fleming wrote in his diary, "I am longing now to reach the Aucas, if God gives me the honor of proclaiming the Name among them. I would gladly give my life for that tribe, if only to see an assembly of those proud, clever, smart people gathering around a table to honor the Son—gladly, gladly, gladly! What more could be given to a life?"

After traveling eighteen days at sea, Jim and Pete arrived in Guayaquil, Ecuador. Again, Pete wrote in his diary, "About half-way up the Guayas River, I finally comprehended that this, this was Ecuador. I felt a tingling sensation for the first time. Jim and I sang quietly, 'Faith of our Fathers, holy faith, we will be true to Thee till death' as the boat pulled into the harbor."[5]

Not long after that, on January 8, 1956, Jim, Pete, and three other missionaries were martyred by the Aucas they loved for Christ's sake. But the missionaries' work was not in vain, for several of their wives later returned to Ecuador and won many of their husbands' murderers to faith in Christ. Jim Elliot and Pete Fleming took up their crosses and followed their Lord—all the way to the place of execution.

In the early 1980s, Colombian guerrillas took captive a young Wycliffe Bible translator named Chet Bitterman. They then issued this ultimatum: "All Wycliffe personnel must leave our country in ten days or we will kill our hostage." The Christian organization replied, "We do not bargain with terrorists or pay ransoms for hostages. We will stay. Our missionary's life is expendable for the cause of Christ."

Shortly thereafter Chet Bitterman was slaughtered. When his mother, Mary Bitterman, of Lancaster, Pennsylvania, heard the news, *Eternity* magazine quoted her quiet response: "There's a lot more involved than the life of our son. There are the lives of thousands of Indians in the jungle who have never heard the story of Jesus."[6]

Why was Chet Bitterman's life expendable for the cause of Christ? Because he had already taken up his cross in obedience to his Lord. How could Mary Bitterman respond so gracefully to the news of her son's death? Because in taking up her own cross, she had died to everything and everyone but Jesus.

YOU CAN LAY DOWN YOUR LIFE FOR CHRIST TODAY

Paul once testified, "I die daily" (1 Cor. 15:31). Elsewhere he claimed, "I have been crucified with Christ; and it is no longer I who live, but

Christ lives in me" (Gal. 2:20). You may never be called on to burn at the stake or be torn apart by wild animals, but you can experience a spiritual martyrdom for Christ each day by surrendering yourself consciously and unconditionally.

If your day is filled with personal plans, you mount the cross by saying, "Lord, my time is really Your time. If You want to interfere with my schedule, I will be flexible." You die to self when a careless driver cuts in front of you and rather than curse him, you breathe this prayer: "Thank You, Lord, for rescuing me from a near accident." You die to self when in business you choose to be honest, even though it costs you money or a promotion. You die to self when you allow your spouse to have his or her way, even when you're convinced he or she is wrong. In some sense, every Christian should be able to say with Paul, "I die daily" (1 Cor. 15:31). Sometimes this is more gutsy than literally burning at the stake.

Some Christians, instead of dying daily, are led astray by others because they fear that their friendships will die. Some are afraid that their careers will die, so they cave in to unethical business practices. Others dread an uncertain future and so nurture in their hearts a love for money.

Bill Harvey spoke for us all when he wrote the following:

> *I must die.*
> *Not waiting till my hair is white*
> *Or falling in a battle fight*
> *Or sleeping on a final night,*
> *But daily.*
>
> *Self must die.*
> *All that self ever hoped to be;*
> *Self dies hard, not easily;*
> *In its place my Lord must see*
> *A corpse.*
>
> *I must die.*
> *Clay I was and clay I'll be;*
> *Let my Potter now mold me,*
> *Then I'll be whatever He*
> *Would wish.*[7]

Everything and everyone has to die. Sadly, that's the law of life. In the spiritual realm, God calls on His children to die daily. When was the last time you took up your cross and followed Jesus? When it comes to your marriage, Jesus asks, "Will you lay down your life for Me?" In your relationships with your children or parents, He asks, "Will you lay down your life for Me?" When you arrive at school or work each day, His question remains, "Will you lay down your life for Me?" Don't presume that you could burn at the stake if you can't die to self-interest now.

Action Steps

Jesus' question, "Will you lay down your life for Me?" implies that He wants us to be more than *willing* to do that. Therefore, the question we should ask in return is not, "Lord, do You want me to lay down my life for You?" but "Lord, *in what way* do You want me to lay down my life for You?"

He may want you to give up your career and leave your comfortable lifestyle to travel to another part of the globe as a missionary. Perhaps God is calling you to prepare for a local church pastoral ministry. Certainly He wants you to dedicate your time and abilities where you are so that people with whom you work might learn of Christ. Possibly for you it would be just like laying down your life if you were to give in generous financial ways to the work of the gospel throughout the world. However Jesus is calling you to lay down your life for Him, obey Him.

Do you have a Savior worth dying for? If you do, then live for Him. Today Jesus calls us to be living sacrifices. Scripture appeals to us as follows: "I urge you therefore, brethren, by the mercies of God, to present your bodies a living and holy sacrifice, acceptable to God, which is your spiritual service of worship" (Rom. 12:1).

Perhaps it would be easier to be a dead sacrifice than a living one. The latter must crawl back on the altar every day. The last dead sacrifice in the Bible was the body of Christ. Now that you have received new life by trusting in Him, sacrifice that life right back to Him. Sacrifice your time to Him. Sacrifice your love to Him. Sacrifice your service to Him. Sacrifice your career to Him.

Jesus still asks, "Will you lay down your life for Me?" That's a question you can answer today in your home, your place of work, your church, and your neighborhood—and in our rapidly changing world, perhaps one day in front of a firing squad.

Study Guide

1. In Genesis 22:1–18 Isaac was willing to die in obedience to his father and ultimately to the Lord. What unanswered questions do you think might have been rushing through Isaac's mind when he realized that his father was preparing to sacrifice him?

2. Read Daniel 3:16–18, in which Shadrach, Meshach, and Abednego were ready to burn to death rather than worship an idol. What do you think made these three men willing to lay down their lives for their Lord?

3. In Daniel 6, Daniel entered a lions' den rather than cease praying to God. Many Christians today fail to pray, even though it is legal. Would these believers be ready to die for Christ if prayer were outlawed?

4. Read Acts 7:54–60, in which Stephen, the first recorded Christian martyr, gave his life for the Lord. Did God answer his dying prayer in verse 60? If so, when?

5. During the persecutions of the first century A.D., Christians said that their blood was the harvest seed that bore fruit in new converts. How does faithfulness to the point of death attract new people to Christ?

6. Read 1 Corinthians 12:3. Suppose you were facing imminent martyrdom, but your persecutors would set you free for saying, "Jesus is accursed." Your spouse and children need you. God would know how you really felt about Christ, and you could confess your faith and plead His forgiveness later. Under these circumstances, why should you choose death rather than say, "Jesus is accursed"?

7. How do these verses encourage you to remain true to Christ to the point of death?

   • Luke 14:26

   • Revelation 2:10

   • Revelation 2:13

   • Revelation 12:11

8. What makes your faith in Christ worth dying for?

9. In what figurative way have you laid down your life for Christ in the last year?

13

AN INTIMATE QUESTION:

"Do you love Me?"
(John 21:15–17)

JASON TUSKES WAS A 17-YEAR-OLD high school honor student who loved to scuba dive. One Tuesday morning he explored an underwater cave near his home in west-central Florida. He planned to celebrate his mother's birthday that evening by going out to dinner with his parents and younger brother.

In the cave, Jason became wedged by a narrow passageway. After struggling in vain to free himself, he unstrapped his yellow air tank, now nearly empty, and unsheathed his diver's knife. On the side of the tank he scratched a final message to his family: "I LOVE YOU MOM, DAD, AND CHRISTIAN."

Then he drowned.[1]

There were so many things Jason could have said, but he chose the words "I love you." Nothing was more important to him than that. No other words could have communicated better to his family the feelings of his heart.

Aren't those the words every human being longs to hear? Children whose parents never say, "I love you" often lack self-esteem. Some people take their own lives because they feel unloved.

Of all the questions Jesus asked in the Gospels, only one was repeated more than once. In three consecutive verses, Christ asked Peter, "Do you love Me?" (John 21:15–17). Jesus could have asked His disciple, "Do you serve Me?" or "Do you speak to others about Me?" or "Do you worship Me?" But Jesus wanted to be more intimate than that.

Still today Jesus' primary question to us is, "Do you love Me?" He doesn't ask, "Do you attend church?" or "Do you tithe?" or "Do you pray?" or "Do you read your Bible?" If we can honestly answer *yes* to His question, "Do you love Me?" then these other areas of spiritual responsibility will take care of themselves.

WHY SHOULD YOU LOVE CHRIST?

One reason you should love Jesus is that *He loves you.* With blood-red ink He penned His dying message to you on a Roman cross, and that message reads, "I LOVE YOU!" As He Himself stated in John 15:13, "Greater love has no one than this, that one lay down his life for his friends."

Harry Bonder, a pastor in Kansas, was awakened at 3 A.M. by two state troopers, who informed him that his son's car had swerved off the road and burst into flames. Eyewitnesses testified that the fire was so intense that there was no way to save the young man. Bonder replied softly, "I think if I had been there, I would have tried." Love for his son would have compelled him to act, even against all odds.

J. Lesslie Newbigin writes, "The love of God can be revealed only by an act. Words alone cannot reveal love. Even if God were to write the words 'God is love' in letters of fire in the clouds, it would not tell us anything. Love must be expressed."[2]

God's love was expressed in the death of Christ. His crucifixion was solid proof that God loves you. Romans 5:8 puts it, "God demonstrates His own love toward us, in that while we were yet sinners, Christ died for us." Because Jesus showed you the greatest of all loves, it only makes sense that you should love Him in return.

Another reason you should love Christ is that *by doing so you fulfill the greatest of all commandments.* A scribe asked Jesus, "What commandment is the foremost of all?" (Mark 12:28). Jesus responded, "You shall love the LORD your God with all your heart, and with all your soul, and with all your mind, and with all your strength" (v. 30). Of course Jesus was referring to God the Father. But Christ also is the Lord God. Since loving Him fulfills the greatest commandment, then failure to love Him must be the worst sin.

Again, your love should go out to Christ because *it will cause you to profit from suffering.* You may be in the furnace of affliction. Perhaps a family member has died, or you have lost your health, or your marriage is disintegrating, or your children are breaking your heart. Sooner or later the faith of every Christian is tested in the crucible of adversity. In such times, perhaps the most often claimed promise in Scripture is Romans 8:28: "God causes all things to work together for good to those who love God."

Mark those last words, "to those who love God." If you don't love Christ, all your pleasures become calluses that harden you against the gospel. But when your heart belongs to Jesus, even feelings of emptiness prepare you for His fullness, life-threatening illnesses build healthy faith, and death itself ushers you into His presence. People who love Christ take all of life's trials as opportunities to reveal their Lord's sufficiency.

HOW SHOULD YOU LOVE CHRIST?

It is one thing to know that you should love Christ. The next step is to learn how best a sinful human being can express that love. The first way is to *love Christ personally*. All love is built on the foundation of a personal relationship. When you fall in love with someone, you want to learn everything you can about him or her. Jesus didn't ask, "Peter, do you love My teachings?" or "Do you love My church?" or "Do you love My Word?" Rather, His question was, "Do you love Me?" (John 21:15–17).

I face the subtle danger of allowing my love for the ministry to serve as a substitute for my love for Christ. I thoroughly enjoy being a pastor. I know it is God's plan for my life, and I'm excited about each day. But sometimes I stop and ask myself, "Is my love focused on Christ or on His work?" If the latter is the case, I have to take steps to redirect my love back to the Lord.

What do you love about being a Christian? The fellowship and friendships of wonderful people, or the assurance of sins forgiven, or the security of your salvation? God does want you to enjoy those benefits, but He does not want them to be the center of your love. That place is reserved for Jesus alone.

The second way is to *love Christ fervently*. When Jesus was interrogated about the most important commandment in life, He forthrightly responded, "You shall love the LORD your God with *all* your heart, and with *all* your soul, and with *all* your mind, and with *all* your strength" (Mark 12:30; italics added). Those four *alls* signify that our love must be absolute for the one we call Lord. There are no limits on our love for Christ. We are to love Him with everything we've got. Isaac Watts captured this idea in his 1707 hymn, "When I Survey the Wondrous Cross":

> *Were the whole realm of nature mine,*
> *That were a present far too small;*
> *Love so amazing, so divine*
> *Demands my soul, my life, my all.*

Charles Spurgeon's fervent love for Christ is evident in this testimony:

> No joy on earth is equal to the bliss of being all taken up with love to Christ. If I had my choice of all the lives

that I could live, I certainly would not choose to be an emperor, nor to be a millionaire, nor to be a philosopher, for power and wealth and knowledge bring with them sorrow. But I would choose to have nothing to do but love my Lord Jesus—nothing, I mean, but to do all things for his sake, and out of love to him.[3]

We are, third, to *love Christ actively*. Paul once commended the Thessalonian believers for their "labor of love" (1 Thess. 1:3). The NIV says a "labor prompted by love." Their love for Christ stimulated them to work hard for Him.

A man in our church has a tremendous business sense. Many times he has been invited to serve as a deacon, but he has always declined. "I'm not spiritual enough," he says.

One time I replied, "But you are spiritual enough, for you love Christ, don't you?" With full assurance he nodded his head yes. So I went on: "The other men on our deacon board aren't theologians. Their all-encompassing qualification for service is that they possess a sincere love for the Lord, just like you!"

Love compelled Jesus to shed His blood on the cross for you. Shouldn't you, therefore, give yourself unconditionally to Him? Jesus allowed Roman soldiers to nail His hands and feet to a criminal's cross for you. Will your hands not work for Him? Will your feet not move for Him? Why do we have many churchgoers today but few servants? Because people have neglected to demonstrate their unconditional love for Christ. If you love Him, show it in acts of service to His cause.

Fourth, we are to *love Christ by faith*. Scripture describes faith as "the conviction of things not seen" (Heb. 11:1). With that in mind, consider this statement from 1 Peter 1:8: "Though you have not seen Him, you love Him." Some people protest that they cannot love Christ, precisely because they have never seen Him. But whenever you love others, faith is involved. You don't know whether they are telling you the truth or deceiving you. You can't see what they will be like in ten years. You don't know whether they will let something in their background, such as child abuse, destroy their relationship with you at some point in the future. But you love them anyway. That's faith!

Harry Rimmer once sent a questionnaire to several hundred women that asked, "Could you love a man you had never seen?" Most responded with a *yes* under certain conditions. Some said that they could love a man they had never seen if they knew he was good and kind. Others said that they could love such a man if he had done some heroic deed. Still others replied that they could love a man without seeing him if he were unselfish and put people ahead of himself.

All those traits apply to the unseen object of our love—Jesus Christ. He is good and kind. He accomplished the most heroic deed in history when He purchased our salvation on Calvary's cross. He also proved His unselfishness when He willingly suffered the wrath of God for the people who murdered Him.

Yes, we can love Christ by faith. The Bible even speaks of "faith working through love" (Gal. 5:6). Notice, faith works! And it works through love. An anonymous Christian expressed it in these words:

> *Jesus, these eyes have never seen*
> *That radiant form of Thine;*
> *The veil of sense hangs dark between*
> *Thy blessed face and mine.*

> *I see Thee not, I hear Thee not,*
> *Yet Thou art oft with me;*
> *And earth hath ne'er so dear a spot*
> *As where I meet with Thee.*

> *Yet, though I have not seen, and still*
> *Must rest in faith alone,*
> *I love Thee, Lord, and always will,*
> *Unseen, but not unknown!*

Fifth, we are to *love Christ unconditionally.* We usually apply that adverb to His love for us. A little girl was introducing a man to each of her dolls by name. He asked, "Which doll is your favorite?" She hesitated, then went into another room, from which she brought out a doll with its hair gone, its nose broken, and a leg missing. The man asked, "Why do you love this doll the most?"

She replied, "Because if I didn't love this doll, no one would."

That's a picture of how Jesus loves us. When Christ laid down His life for us, sin had already disfigured us and made us unlovely. When we had no beauty to offer Him, He loved us unconditionally.

So love Jesus unconditionally in return. I've observed many people who are full of love for Christ when they are healthy, prosperous, and enjoying life. But then adversity strikes. A family member dies prematurely. A wedding engagement is broken. A baby is born deformed. An accident paralyzes a loved one. A blood transfusion infects a family member with the HIV virus. Slowly love turns to bitterness.

Granted, these problems defy our understanding, and it's natural to grieve over them. But if resentment replaces love for Christ, our hearts betray a conditional love. In Ephesians 6:24, Paul wrote, "Grace be with all those who love our Lord Jesus Christ with a love incorruptible." Other versions translate it "an undying love" or "a never-diminishing love." It is an unconditional love for Christ.

The sixteenth-century Jesuit missionary Francis Xavier described such love in these words:

> *Why, O blessed Jesus Christ*
> *Should I not love You well?*
> *Not for the sake of winning heaven*
> *Or of escaping hell.*
>
> *Not with the hope of gaining things,*
> *Nor seeking a reward;*
> *But as You proved Your love to me,*
> *O ever-loving Lord.*
>
> *And so I love You, and will love,*
> *And all Your praises sing;*
> *Because You are my loving God,*
> *And my eternal King.*

How Can You Test Your Love for Christ?

The New Testament offers two tests of our love for Christ. One is *love for our fellow Christians*. First John 4:20 warns, "If someone says, 'I love God,' and hates his brother, he is a liar; for the one who does not love his brother whom he has seen, cannot love God whom he has not seen."

Before every meal and at bedtime each day I take a simple test to measure the amount of sugar in my bloodstream. As a diabetic, I must do this to maintain good control of the disease. I prick my finger with a lancet, squeeze out a drop of blood onto a test strip, insert the strip into a meter, and in a few seconds receive a readout of my sugar level.

Before these meters were invented I thought I could estimate the amount of sugar in my body by the way I felt. Now I know that's impossible. Often I'm surprised by the result of my test scores. If it is above my desired range, I'll take an insulin injection to bring it down. If the meter is wrong and my sugar level is actually low, the added insulin will send me into shock. But after thousands of tests, my meter has never been wrong. I have learned to rely on it and disregard my feelings.

How do you know that you love Christ? You believe you love Him, but you want confirmation. Then look at God's spiritual "meter." Your love for other Christians is the measure of your love for Christ.

The second test of love is seen in *a controlled life*. This is the message of 2 Corinthians 5:14: "The love of Christ controls us." The phrase "the love of Christ" could refer to Jesus' love for us or our love for Him. Commentators argue over these alternatives. But why exclude one in favor of the other? Christ's love for us is intended to inspire a similar love for Him in return. And both loves control our behavior.

Is your spiritual life out of control? Are you living recklessly, even though you profess to love Christ? Has sin obliterated the last trace of holiness in your life? Then don't claim that you love the Lord, for you don't. Jesus said, "If you love Me, you will keep My commandments. . . . He who has My commandments and keeps them, he it is who loves Me. . . . If anyone loves Me, he will keep My word" (John 14:15, 21, 23).

If your so-called love for Christ doesn't control your behavior, consider whom you really love. Authentic love for Christ always brings a person under His control. Scripture makes no exceptions.

Action Steps

Today Jesus asks you, as He asked Peter, "Do you love Me?" This is such a crucial question, for if you don't love Christ, you will be eternally lost. Jesus said to the Jews of His day, "If God were your Father, you would love Me" (John 8:42). This implies that people without love for Christ have Satan as their spiritual father. Paul went so far as to say, "If any one does not love the Lord, let him be accursed" (1 Cor. 16:22). And James spoke about "the kingdom which He promised to those who love Him" (James 2:5).

It is not enough to be a member of the church. Many church members do not love Christ, and they are lost. One might say, "I thought faith, not love, was the one human ingredient necessary for salvation." True. But many people mistake faith for mere mental assent. God's Word teaches that faith inspires love for the Christ in whom we trust (see Gal. 5:6; 1 Thess. 1:3).

Often I listen to people who lack assurance of salvation. They know the gospel and believe in Christ, but they wonder if their faith is genuine. They don't want to be duped into damnation. To guide them in their quest, I ask, "Do you love Christ?" That brings them back to square one and helps them discern the authenticity of their faith.

What if you can't honestly say, as Peter, "Lord, You know all things; You know that I love You" (John 21:17)? What if you are forced to admit, "Jesus, I've wasted love on unworthy objects"? Then *commit* yourself to loving Christ. Love is an act of the will, not a feeling. You can choose to love the Lord Jesus. He Himself implied that when He declared that the greatest commandment was this: "You shall love the LORD your

God with all your heart, and with all your soul, and with all your mind, and with all your strength" (Mark 12:30).

Jesus said, "Where your treasure is, there will your heart be also" (Matt. 6:21). That sounds backwards, doesn't it? We might expect the verse to read, "Where your heart is, there will your treasure be also." But no, first we make something our treasure, then our hearts follow it.

Therefore, make Jesus your treasure by giving Him first place in your life. Each day commit yourself to speak to Him in prayer, to listen to His voice in Scripture, to meditate on His attributes, and to rejoice in His love. Then your heart will love Him too. You have His promise.

Study Guide

1. Jesus asked Peter, "Do you love Me more than these?" (John 21:15). Some interpreters think that He meant, "Do you love Me more than these fishing nets from which you have earned your living?" What in your life (career, hobby, recreation, and so on) most competes with Christ for your love?

2. Why do you think Peter was grieved when Jesus asked him the third time, "Do you love Me?" (v. 17). Why didn't he grieve the first or second time (vv. 15–16)? What light, if any, does John 13:38 shed on this exchange?

3. Jesus could have asked Peter, "Are you sorry for denying Me?" or "Do you promise never to do it again?" or "Will you serve Me?" or "Do you love the lambs I want you to tend?" But Jesus simply asked three times, "Do you love Me?" Why did Jesus place so much emphasis on loving Him?

4. Give a personal reason why you love Christ.

5. Is it possible to genuinely trust in Christ for salvation and not unconditionally love Him? Explain your answer.

6. How would you respond if a friend admits, "I know I should love Christ, but I just don't. You can't expect me to manufacture love out of nothing"?

7. One practical way to show love for Christ is to love others. What do these passages teach about Christian love?

   • Matthew 5:43–46

   • John 13:34–35

   • John 15:13

   • 1 Thessalonians 4:9

   • 1 John 3:16

   • 1 John 4:7–8

8. In what sense can every Christian obey Jesus' three commands, "Tend My lambs" (John 21:15), "Shepherd My sheep" (v. 16), and "Tend My sheep" (v. 17)? Does there seem to be any difference between these commands?

9. Psalm 23:1, John 10:11, Hebrews 13:20, 1 Peter 2:25, and 1 Peter 5:4 all have a common denominator. What is it? How does it encourage you to obey Jesus' command, "Shepherd My sheep" (John 21:16)?

10. In John 10:11–18. what is the difference between a shepherd and a hired hand?

11. Jesus taught that Christians are the sheep of His spiritual flock. What characteristics of sheep are emphasized in these verses?

    • Psalm 119:176

    • Isaiah 53:6

    • Luke 15:4

    • John 10:27

Endnotes

CHAPTER 1

1. R. V. G. Tasker, *The Gospel According to St. Matthew* (Grand Rapids: Eerdmans, 1961), 157.
2. Albert Schweitzer, *The Quest for the Historical Jesus,* trans. W. Montgomery (New York: Macmillan, 1961).
3. Augustus H. Strong, *Systematic Theology* (Old Tappen, N.J.: Revell, 1979).

CHAPTER 2

1. T. R. Glover, *The Jesus of History* (London, 1917), 192.
2. Donald Grey Barnhouse, *Man's Ruin* (Grand Rapids: Eerdmans, 1952), 25.

CHAPTER 3

1. Leonard Ravenhill, *Why Revival Tarries* (Minneapolis: Bethany Fellowship, 1979), 32.
2. Charles Swindoll, *Growing Strong in the Seasons of Life* (Portland, Ore.: Multnomah, 1983), 94.
3. C. S. Lewis, *Surprised by Joy* (New York: Harcourt, Brace and Co., 1955), 211–24.

Chapter 4

1. *Alcoholics Anonymous* (New York: Alcoholics Anonymous World Services, Inc., 1976), 46.
2. Michael P. Green, *Illustrations for Biblical Preaching* (Grand Rapids: Baker, 1982), 140.
3. J. I. Packer, *God's Words* (Downers Grove, Ill.: InterVarsity, 1981), 129.
4. Al Munger, *Time Out!* ed. Clint and Mary Beckwith (Ventura, Calif.: Evergreen, 1989), 77–78.
5. Louisa Stead, "'Tis So Sweet to Trust in Jesus," 1882.
6. *Sword of the Lord,* March 13, 1981, 16.
7. Lidie Edmunds, "No Other Plea," 19th century.

Chapter 5

1. Charles Spurgeon, *2200 Quotations from the Writings of Charles H. Spurgeon,* ed. Tom Carter (Grand Rapids: Baker, 1988), 118.
2. James M. Boice, "Galatians," in *The Expositor's Bible Commentary,* ed. Frank E. Gaebelein (Grand Rapids: Zondervan, 1976), 10:467.

Chapter 6

1. Daniel R. Schwartz, "Pontius Pilate," in *The Anchor Bible Dictionary,* ed. David N. Freedman (New York: Doubleday, 1992), 5:395–401.
2. I. Howard Marshall, *The Gospel of Luke: A Commentary on the Greek Text* (Grand Rapids: Eerdmans, 1978), 554.
3. Walter Bauer, *A Greek-English Lexicon of the New Testament,* 2d ed., trans. W. F. Arndt and F. W. Gingrich, rev. F. W. Gingrich and F. W. Danker (Chicago: University of Chicago Press, 1979), 511.
4. Ibid., 568.
5. Gerhard Kittel and Gerhard Friedrich, eds., *Theological Dictionary of the New Testament,* 1 vol. ed., trans., abr., G. W. Bromiley (Grand Rapids: Eerdmans, 1985), 687.
6. W. S. Reid, "Repentance," in *Evangelical Dictionary of Theology,* ed. Walter A. Elwell (Grand Rapids: Baker, 1984), 936.

Chapter 7

1. For example, note the emphatic comments made by John F. Walvoord in *Matthew: Thy Kingdom Come* (Chicago: Moody, 1974), 102–4.

2. George Eldon Ladd, *The Presence of the Future* (Grand Rapids: Eerdmans, 1974).

CHAPTER 8

1. William S. LaSor, "Towers," in *The International Standard Bible Encyclopedia,* ed. Geoffrey W. Bromiley (Grand Rapids: Eerdmans, 1988), 4:881.
2. William Barclay, *The Gospel of Luke,* in the Daily Study Bible series (Philadelphia: Westminster, 1956), 203.
3. W. E. Vine, Merrill F. Unger, and William White, *Vine's Complete Expository Dictionary of Old and New Testament Words* (Nashville: Nelson, 1985), 171.
4. Walter Bauer, *A Greek-English Lexicon of the New Testament,* 2d ed., trans. W. F. Arndt and F. W. Gingrich, rev. F. W. Gingrich and F. W. Danker (Chicago: University of Chicago Press, 1979), 171.
5. See H. L. Drumwright, "Crucifixion," in *The Zondervan Pictorial Encyclopedia of the Bible,* ed. Merrill C. Tenney (Grand Rapids: Zondervan, 1976), 1:1040–42.
6. G. Campbell Morgan, *The Gospel According to Luke* (New York: Revell, 1931), 175.

CHAPTER 9

1. Charles Spurgeon, *2200 Quotations from the Writings of Charles H. Spurgeon,* ed. Tom Carter (Grand Rapids: Baker, 1988), 106.
2. C. J. Wright, *Jesus the Revelation of God* (London, 1950), 164, cited by Leon Morris, *The Cross in the New Testament* (Grand Rapids: Eerdmans, 1965), 149.
3. Charles Haddon Spurgeon, *Spurgeon's Devotional Bible* (Grand Rapids: Baker, 1977), 607.

CHAPTER 10

1. Walter Bauer, *A Greek-English Lexicon of the New Testament,* 2d ed., trans. W. F. Arndt and F. W. Gingrich, rev. F. W. Gingrich and F. W. Danker (Chicago: University of Chicago Press, 1979), 249.
2. Frederick C. Mish, ed., *Merriam Webster's Collegiate Dictionary,* 10th ed. (Springfield, Mass.: Merriam-Webster, 1993), 255.
3. Howard Cleveland in *Baker's Dictionary of Theology,* ed. Everett F. Harrison (Grand Rapids: Baker, 1960), 140.
4. Charles Spurgeon, *2200 Quotations from the Writings of Charles H. Spurgeon,* ed. Tom Carter (Grand Rapids: Baker, 1988), 45.

5. See H. L. Ellison, "Jonah," in *The Expositor's Bible Commentary* (Grand Rapids: Zondervan, 1976), 7:389. Also, Leslie C. Allen, *The Books of Joel, Obadiah, Jonah, and Micah* (Grand Rapids: Eerdmans, 1976), 234.
6. Bill Bright, *Witnessing Without Fear* (San Bernadino, Calif.: Here's Life, 1987), 141–42.

CHAPTER 11

1. William Coleman, *Christianity Today,* 23 September 1977, 38.
2. Ray C. Stedman, *The Death of Death* (Palo Alto, Calif.: Discovery Papers, April 14, 1968), 3.

CHAPTER 12

1. James Reapsome, *Christian History* 9, no. 3, 37.
2. John O. Gooch, *Christian History* 9, no. 3, 31.
3. Ibid., 33.
4. H. B. Swete, *The Gospel According to St. Mark* (London, 1913; Grand Rapids, 1956).
5. Elisabeth Elliot, *Through the Gates of Splendor* (New York: Harper and Row, 1957).
6. *Eternity,* May 1981, 10.
7. *Sword of the Lord,* 9 October 1981, 15.

CHAPTER 13

1. Larry James, *Leadership,* summer 1990, 49.
2. J. Lesslie Newbigin, *Sin and Salvation* (London, 1956), 71.
3. Charles Spurgeon, *2200 Quotations from the Writings of Charles H. Spurgeon,* ed. Tom Carter (Grand Rapids: Baker, 1988), 123.